Tradition » Passion » Perfection

John Lamond is a Master of Malt and author of several
books, including *The Malt Whisky File* (now in its
seventh edition). He contributes to international
consumer magazines and industry journals, has
conducted whiskey tastings worldwide, and lectured for
the Wine & Spirit Education Trust for over twenty years.
He also created the Scotch Whisky Trail Certificate
Course, the world's first Scotch whisky evening class.

Princeton Architectural Press
37 East Seventh Street
New York, NY 10003
Visit our website at www.papress.com

Conceived and produced by
Elwin Street Productions
3 Percy Street
London W1T 1DE
www.elwinstreet.com

Illustrations: Tonwen Jones
Photo credits: Corbis: pp. 61, 73; Maker's Mark: p. 79;
Photolibrary.com: p. 49; Getty: p. 95

Library of Congress Cataloging-in-Publication Data
Lamond, John.
Whiskey / John Lamond. — First edition.
pages cm — (Instant expert)
Includes index.
ISBN 978-1-61689-216-6 (alk. paper)
1. Whiskey. I. Title.
TP605.L38 2013
663'.52—dc23
2013015061

WHISKEY

John Lamond

Princeton Architectural Press, New York

Contents

Why be an expert about whiskey?

Whiskey is the greatest drink in the world—the stuff of legend, of healing, of friendship and companionship. In old Gaelic it was literally "the water of life." No other spirit offers such finesse, such elegance, such complexity, or such value. With all the excellent choices available, no one should settle for a whiskey they don't enjoy. It just starts with knowing what is out there.

Scotch whisky is spelled "whisky" and must be from Scotland to be called scotch. With Irish whiskey—which has had perhaps an even longer history—the word is spelled "whiskey." This spelling is used elsewhere in the world, including the US, with its ryes and bourbons, first brewed by pioneering settlers from Scotland and Ireland.

There is an enthusiasm about whiskey that did not exist 30 years ago, and which has enabled a great deal of research into what goes on inside the cask. As a result, the quality of spirit now being bottled has never been higher. The boutique distilleries, in particular, are benefiting from this new research and knowledge, as they are able to experiment with small amounts of spirit and unusual casks, and so they in turn impart new information to the large distilleries. Thus within an already wide range of whiskey, there are different ages, finishes, and experimental bottlings for you to sample and enjoy.

Generally, but not necessarily, the younger a whiskey, the coarser, more cerealy flavored it is going to be as it has not yet had time to lose its hard and youthful rough edges nor had time to assimilate softer, mature, oak characters. Some whiskeys, such as Glen Grant or Glenfiddich, only start to come into their own after 18 years, while bourbons, Canadian or American ryes, Indian or Australian whiskeys, because of their warmer maturation conditions, mature relatively quickly. In fact, it is very unusual for these to survive in the cask much longer than 15 years simply because of the heat. If one of these hot-country whiskeys has been bottled in excess of 15 years of age, you can be sure that particular care has been taken over these casks while they aged, as the company's reputation hangs on your appreciation of their whiskeys.

Aged whiskey is valuable. Glenfiddich 50 Years Old, for example, is only the second vatting (the term for the blending process) ever made. The first was produced from nine casks laid down between 1937 and 1939 by Glenfiddich founder David Grant—one for each of his grandchildren as a thank you for helping him build the distillery. The usual retail price for a bottle is about $13,000, although in 2009 one sold at auction in New York for $38,000. Another very valuable whiskey is the Dalmore 62 Years Old, which could be your drink of aspiration at $43,000. Only 12 bottles were produced and one of these was bought—and drunk—in a hotel bar in London two years ago. Should you acquire one, please give me a shout when you open the bottle if you feel in need of some good company.

These are unique and special products often made by craftsmen decades ago. An old vintage cannot be repeated and will be a biography of the seasons of that year. Whiskey from colder climates like Scotland and Ireland will invariably improve with age, although those from warmer countries like America are rarely kept more than 15 years because of the heat.

The range of flavors is tantalizing. At one end of the spectrum there is the delicate, unpeated Glengoyne where the barley is air dried. The flavor is of green apples and sweet licorice turning to linseed and almonds; at the other there is the huge smokey, seaweed pungency of Laphroaig. In between we have a whole rainbow of styles from shortbread to syrup to Asian spices to smoked trout.

In this book I have picked out some of the great whiskeys of today, my personal favorites from all over the world, for you to savor and enjoy.

» Fundamentals

Whiskey's ingredients

Whiskey is made from a small number of ingredients —grain, yeast, and water—and the process itself is relatively straightforward. Each distillery combines the raw materials using tried and tested production techniques to create the "water of life."

Grain

Whiskey is made from the cereal grains barley, corn, rye, and wheat. The grain used defines the characteristics of a whiskey. Having a high level of starch, most barley grown today is used in the production of whiskey and beer. Single malt whiskey is made from 100 percent fully malted grains of barley. All other whiskeys are made from a mix of different proportions of these four grains.

Yeast

During production, the single-celled organism yeast is added to the porridge-like mash and feeds on its sugars that are transformed into alcohol and carbon dioxide. There are many distillers' yeasts and brewers' yeasts to choose from and each will have a different affect on a whiskey's character.

Water

Every distillery needs a plentiful local source of water to produce whiskey because water is added and removed at different stages of a whiskey's production. In Kentucky, most water is hard, having filtered through limestone, which adds minerals to the water, making enzyme action during the mashing process more efficient as well as influencing the flavor formation. Water in the Scottish Highlands is mostly soft flowing through granite as well as over peat and heather. Soft water has a low calcium content that enables the yeast added during fermentation to make a strong start.

Wood

Even though not strictly an ingredient, the wood used to make the casks in which whiskey matures influences the spirit's complexity. Many whiskey experts argue that during maturation the cask contributes up to 70 percent of the flavor and character of a whiskey. The wood used for casks today is mainly American white oak (*Quercus alba*). For a whiskey to be deemed bourbon it has to be matured in new casks of white oak and the spirit extracts vanillin from the wood, which gives a sweet vanilla note to bourbon. Bourbon casks are also charred to different levels enabling the spirit to access fully the flavors in the semi-porous wood. Scottish, Irish, and Japanese distilleries reuse bourbon and sherry casks during maturation.

Peat

Peat is partially carbonized plant material that is usually found in waterlogged areas. Twelve percent of Scotland's landmass is peat land. Water that flows over peat absorbs some of its earthy characteristics but not as much as a whiskey in which the barley has been malted over burning peat that gives distinctive earthy and smoky aromas and flavors. In Scotland some peats include delayed seaweed that gives a salty, iodine characteristic to a spirit.

Making whiskey

The process of making whiskey has remained unchanged from generation to generation following the main stages of malting, mashing, fermentation, distillation, and maturation to produce the most complex spirit known to humankind.

Malting

The first step in whiskey production is to soak barley in water for several days and then spread on the malting floor. As the grains start to germinate, called the "green malt," they are transferred to the kiln, at exactly the appropriate time where a higher temperature prevents further germination. This step retains the grain's starch content that will be turned into sugars at the next stage of production. Some distilleries in Scotland, Ireland, and Japan dry the barley over burning peat that adds to the aromas and flavors of the finished whiskey. The malted barley is then milled to coarse flour known as "grist."

Malt whiskey is made from 100 percent malted barley while grain whiskey may contain a percentage of malted barley. Today, commercial malting companies usually undertake the malting process, often producing malted barley to a distillery's exact specification. A few distilleries in Scotland still malt their own barley (such as Bowmore, see page 50).

Mashing

The grist is mixed with hot water to form a mash that is then stirred at high temperatures releasing enzymes that convert the grains' starch to sugars, which dissolve into the hot water. The remaining liquid (now called the "wort") cools and is drained into large wooden or steel vessels.

Fermentation

As the wort enters the fermenting vessel, yeast is added. Fermentation begins, rapidly converting the sugars in the wort into alcohol. The wort, now known as the "wash," contains around 7 to 10 percent alcohol and is ready for distillation.

Distillation

The process of distillation can take place in either a pot still or a continuous still. Because alcohol boils at a lower temperature than water, the wash is heated and the spirit is drawn off as a vapor that rises into a condenser. The alcohol is then condensed back into a liquid that is collected.

Pot still distillation

Malt whiskey is distilled in a pot still. It is twice—sometimes three times—distilled in stills that look like big copper onions. The copper helps the separation of the spirit from the water. In the first distillation, the heating cooks out the crude alcohols and other elements. The results, known as "low wines," are passed into the spirit still, similar in shape but smaller than the pot still because it does not need to deal with the same quantities. Low wines contain 21 percent alcohol.

The second distillation produces three distinct liquids or condensates: The first of these is called "foreshots" or "heads," the second is the "heart," and the last is called "feints" or "tails." Foreshots are very high in strength (75 to 80 percent alcohol), mildly toxic containing some methanol, while the feints are low in alcohol. Foreshots and feints go back into the pot still to lend character to the next batch of distillation. The heart (containing between 63 to 72 percent alcohol) goes into casks for maturation.

Column still distillation

Grain whiskey is produced in a column still (often known as a continuous or patent still.) The continuous still was patented in 1831 by Aeneas Coffey, a former Inspector-General of Excise in Ireland. Grain whiskey distillation is much more efficient: it produces far greater volumes than pot still distillation but produces a more refined, less characterful spirit and so tends to be used for blends mixed with small amounts of malt whiskey. Grain whiskey will often use a mix of malted and unmalted barley and other grains such as maize, rye, or wheat. Bourbon, rye, Tennessee, and Canadian whiskey, and grain spirit for blending Scotch whisky are distilled in column stills.

Maturation

Whiskey was not aged systematically at a distillery until the end of the 19th century. Today distillers take a more scientific approach. At this stage the spirit, called the "new make," must mature in an oak cask for a minimum of three years before it can be called Scotch whisky. The legal definition of bourbon requires that this spirit be matured in new American oak casks.

Scotch whisky is matured in oak casks that have previously contained bourbon or sherry and the residues within these casks affect the flavor and color of the maturing spirit. Sometimes port, Madeira, or even rum casks have been used for maturation and some distillers have even experimented with Sauternes and claret casks. The

How strong is whiskey?

Alcohol by volume (ABV) is the standard used worldwide to measure the amount of alcohol (as a percentage) in an alcoholic beverage. During distillation the alcohol level varies enormously. The foreshots, for example, are high in strength, about 75–80% ABV, and are set aside to be used in the next distillation. After distillation the new make is about 70% ABV. In Scotland, the spirit is diluted with water to 63% ABV before being put in casks for maturation. American whiskey is barrelled at 53–55% ABV while in Ireland it is 62–75% ABV. As the whiskey matures, alcohol and water evaporate which is called the "angels' share" in Scotland. After emptying a cask, the dregs are called the "devil's cut." After maturation a cask's strength may vary from 57–65% ABV. Some powerful cask strength whiskeys are available. Most whiskey is diluted to 40% ABV before bottling.

expansion and contraction of the cask due to seasonal changes in temperature affects the spirit's maturation. Some harsh spirit flavors may be exhaled through the semi-porous oak cask while the natural aromas of the local environment, such as seaweed, salty sea air, can be absorbed into the cask.

As a whiskey matures, evaporation also causes the cask to lose alcoholic strength and volume, and to absorb oxygen through the cask. The amount of whiskey lost during maturation depends on the temperature and humidity and the microclimate within the warehouse where maturation takes place. In high temperatures, the whiskey absorbs the flavors from the cask more rapidly.

Casks are often left considerably longer than three years before the bottler decides that it is ready to blended and bottled. Most single malts, for example, mature for at least 8 to 15 years before bottling. Bourbons and ryes, however, are ready after two years.

Words from the wise

Andy Davidson Director,
Glencairn Crystal, UK

» The tasting experience

When I drink whiskey, I'll always want to get the most from it—which means using a Glencairn glass.

It's robust and comfortable in the hand and allows an ease of drinking not associated with traditional nosing copitas. The wide bowl allows for the fullest appreciation of the whiskey's color and allows the development of the drink's aromas, while the solid base is designed to be easy on the hand, and also to help in preventing accidental spillage.

You should give the elements in the whiskey time to open out before nosing it, inhaling and identifying as many of the characters present as you are able. Then, the addition of a small splash of water will release the esters and aldehydes (organic compounds) and cause the aroma to expand like a sponge. Only then should you taste. Your palate will confirm everything that your nose has already told you—with the addition of texture in your mouth and the length of the whiskey's flavor.

Types of whiskey

Single malt: Distilled from 100 percent malted barley, a single malt is always the product of one distillery.

Blended malt whiskey: A blend of two or more single malt whiskeys.

Grain whiskey: Contains unmalted barley or other malted and unmalted grains. It has a smoother and lighter flavor. Used mainly for blending.

Blended Scotch whisky: A blend of a single malt and grain whiskys from different distilleries.

Irish whiskey: Column stills and pot stills are both used in distillation. Usually corn is distilled in column still with malted and unmalted barley in pot still. The pot still mash has 40 to 45 percent malted barley. Irish whiskey is triple distilled and matured for three yeas.

Bourbon whiskey: The mash is legally required to have at least 51 percent corn grain. Bourbon must be matured in new, charred white oak barrels for two years.

Tennessee whiskey: A bourbon-style spirit that undergoes filtration through sugar maple charcoal.

Rye whiskey: Made from a mash of not less than 51 percent rye. Matured in charred oak barrels.

Corn whiskey: Distilled from a mash of not less than 80 percent corn. Not aged in charred oak barrels. No minimum maturation period is set.

Canadian whiskey: Mostly rye blended with a neutral base spirit. Bourbon or corn whiskey may be blended. Matured for a minimum of three years in pre-used casks.

Appreciating whiskey

It takes practice to appreciate whiskey. The more you taste whiskey—try to concentrate on each tasting—you will be able to identify and appreciate its aromas and flavors. With practice, you will also be able to identify the country of origin of the oak, learn to associate certain fruity notes with a particular distillery, or even detect a change of distiller.

Considering the color

Hold a glass against a white wall or a sheet of white paper and look at the color. Color gives a clue to the type of cask used; pale golden colors suggest the whiskey was matured in bourbon casks while darker colors indicate sherry casks. Swirl the glass and look at the whiskey's "legs." They give a clue to its age and style. An aged and full-bodied whiskey will have longer legs than a younger, lighter-bodied style.

Using your Nose

A Master Blender uses his nose to make his selection from the aromas of the whiskeys. Your nose is a far more sensitive organ than your palate. Professional distillers sometimes work only with their nose not tasting the whiskey. Smell or "nose" the whiskey and note what you experience: has the aroma the sweetness of malt, is it smoky and fragrant, or is it salty and seaweedy?

Training your palate

The taste of a whiskey should merely confirm everything your nose has already told you. Develop your palate by embarking on a little extra research in the laboratory of your armchair. Take a sip of the whiskey neat and let the mouth feel the whiskey's body: is it big, rich, creamy, smooth, soft, or gentle. Remember there are no right or wrong tastes. We each have a unique palate and we all taste things differently.

Although each cask imposes a slightly different fingerprint on its contents to that of its neighbours, the core characteristics of a distillery's make are there in every cask. Highland Park, for example, always smells distinctly of honey, heather, and vanilla; Glenrothes has notes of orange, honey, and butterscotch; and Caol Ila has embers of burnt heather roots on the shoreline. Each of these flavors should be identifiable with a little practice. Experiment to identify and enjoy them yourself.

Savoring the finish

The lingering flavor of the whiskey in the mouth after it has been swallowed is called the "finish." Think about a whiskey's aftertaste. Does the maltiness and smokiness linger? Is there a long lingering finish? Is the finish short and crisp? You are left with a moment to think before writing a tasting note, the only way to remember your response to a whiskey.

Drew Smith Author of *Oyster, A World History*, London

» Traditional partners for whiskey

021

Personally I like drinking whiskey on its own—all the cooking and artistry has already been done at the distillery and I prefer to taste it as it is, with a splash of water. But that's not to say that whiskey and food cannot be successfully combined, and there are many traditional pairings that are commonly served in the whiskey-drinking cultures of the world.

One example is a dish that might be called surf and turf, found on the west coast of Scotland where the fishermen would traditionally have a dram of malt whiskey with their oysters—not to the side but poured on the shell like we do today with Tabasco.

The Japanese and other Asian cultures often drink whiskey for choice in restaurants. There is a certain affinity to raw fish, to rice, to cuisine that was originally designed around warm saké or shochu. Elsewhere in the world whiskey is usually drunk apart, before or after the meal.

Serving whiskey

Whiskey deserves care, attention, and delicacy in its serving. Even a simple blend often contains whiskeys created decades ago by artisans who are now no longer with us. A single malt is the epitome of that distillery's production, and so deserves respect and reverence. While a good-sized tumbler may suffice for every day, the best whiskey deserves the best glassware.

The right glass

The glass should be large enough to take a good measure so that the aromas gather above the liquid in the bowl. The spirit should breathe. You should be able to smell all the subtleties released in the pouring. Glass is the first choice for the obvious reason that it allows you to appreciate the mellow depths of color in what you are drinking. Recently fashions have moved away from traditional cut crystal to clear tulip-shaped glasses. Color and fragrance are all.

« The Glencairn Whiskey glass (left) and the Vinum Single Malt glass (right)

Scotland's Glencairn Crystal developed their Glencairn Whiskey Glass in 2001. This is now widely used in the world's best whiskey bars. This glass concentrates the aromas into a narrow space towards the lip of the glass, focusing the whiskey experience in a very accurate way.

The renowned Austrian glass producer Georg Riedel designed his Vinum Single Malt glass in the mid-1990s. This has a flared lip, which delivers the spirit to the front of the tongue, emphasizing the sweetness and creaminess of the first taste of the

Glasses and measures

In whiskey terms, many measures are somewhat indeterminate in exact quantity. In the UK, the old standard pub measures of anything from a sixth to a quarter of a gill (a gill is equal to a quarter of a pint, or 142.07 ml), were replaced in 1994 by multiples of 25 ml. Historically, the Scots pint was larger than its English counterpart, the Scots variety being equal to one third of an imperial gallon, so that a Scots gill was always a good measure. A "dram" in a public house can be any one of the measures listed above, but a "dram" in a private home can be anything from a splash, which merely dampens the bottom of the glass, to great tumblers full of whiskey. A "glass" or "gless" is normally accepted to be a double measure in a public house or a large dram in a private home.

whiskey. Wilson and Morgan of Edinburgh produce an undecorated tasting glass for the connoisseur, designed for single malts, that is as fat as a Michelin man and features a petal rim, plus a hat for keeping in the aromas. The whiskey in your glass has taken many years to reach such a pinnacle of perfection, so you shouldn't miss out on the full appreciation of it by serving it in a container, which does not do it justice.

Matching whiskey with food

Whiskey can be a great accompaniment to food. Cheese, especially, goes well with whiskey: Highland Scotch Whiskies with hard ewe's milk cheeses like Manchego or Provolone; Bourbon with a rich, mature Gouda or even a mature cheddar; Canadian or American Rye—or even a big, smoky Islay—with a blue cheese such as Stilton, Lanark Blue, or Rocquefort; Campbeltown with feta… The experimentation is also great fun.

The whole art of matching food with whiskey is making sure that the whiskey does not swamp the flavors of the food—and vice versa. Often this throws up unusual and unexpected partners.

I have seen Macallan 12 Fine Oak matched with seared scallops with fettuccini; Glen Grant 16 Years Old with smoked salmon; Ben Riach 16 Years Old Sauternes Finish inspirationally matched with a leg of lamb stuffed with fruit and spices; Glen Elgin 1975 with a summer fruit salad; king prawns and an olive tapenade with Isle of Jura Superstition; fried oysters with Maker's Mark; and char-grilled steak with Wild Turkey 101. The list is almost endless and only restricted by your imagination.

»Scotch whisky

Single malts

A single malt Scotch whisky is a malt whisky produced from one distillery. It must be aged in Scotland for all of its life and, following the 2009 legislation, must be bottled in Scotland.

Speyside

Scotland's Golden Triangle; the area into which is squeezed almost half of all Scotland's malt whisky distilleries. In the summer of 2010, there were 92 operating malt whisky distilleries in Scotland; of these, 47 are Speyside malts. Speyside's malts are the sweetest in Scotland, the peating levels are generally lower than other areas and sherry casks feature most frequently in the maturation process, a practice that enhances the richness of its whiskies.

Aberlour distillery

Aberlour, Banffshire

Tel: +44(0)1340 881249, www.aberlour.co.uk

Formerly called "Charlestown of Aberlour." the village has now simplified its name to "Aberlour." The distillery's water supply comes from St. Drostan's well, so-named because the early Christian saint baptized converts with its waters.

» **Aberlour a'Bunadh**
Bottled at cask strength and without chill-filtration, a process that standardizes the spirit, but can damage

the flavors, a'Bunadh (which, from the Gaelic, means "original") has been matured exclusively in oloroso sherry casks. This sweetens the whisky and results in a big-bodied, mature and darkly nutty aroma of cooking apples and oranges, while the flavor is rich with citrus and cocoa-flavored peat notes.

BenRiach distillery

Nr. Elgin, Moray

Tel: +44(0)1343 862888,
www.benriachdistillery.co.uk

Opened in 1898, just before the market crashed, the distillery did not open again until 1965. Bought by private investors in 2004, the floor malting (see page 48) was in use until 1999, but could be reactivated. The single malt has been restyled as "The BenRiach."

» **The BenRiach 12 Years Old**
Aromas of apples, flowering heather, honey and vanilla supported by a soft peat touch are followed by a silky, medium-sweet flavor of apple and peach that finishes long, elegant and spicy with a note of milk chocolate.

Benromach distillery

Forres, Moray

Tel: +44(0)1309 675968, www.benromach.com

The distillery has had many owners in its time; it is now owned by Elgin Whisky Merchants, Gordon & MacPhail. Built in 1898 to a design by famed distillery architect Charles Doig, the building has high-pitched gables and narrow, mullioned windows in the Scots vernacular style of the 17th century.

» Benromach Traditional

Medium-bodied and medium-sweet with malty cereals, citrus and soft smoke, followed by a medium-sweet flavor of good body with honey and spicy background peat, which has just a slight medicinal hint.

Glendullan distillery

Dufftown, Banffshire

Tel: +44(0)1340 820250

This was the last distillery to be built in Dufftown in the 19th century and prompted the epithet "Rome was built on seven hills, but Dufftown was built on seven stills."

» Glendullan 16 Years Old Centenary bottling

A classic, and much under-rated, whisky. With notes of new-cut grass, ripe pineapple and peach, this is an elegant mouthful of crème brûlée, toffee, coffee and a delicate underlay of peat on the finish.

Glen Elgin distillery

Longmorn, nr. Elgin, Moray

Tel: +44(0)1343 860212

When this was built, it was the last distillery to be built in Speyside in the 19th century—and there was not another built in the area until 1958.

» Glen Elgin 16 Years Old

A new bottling at cask strength of 58.5 percent a.b.v., this has mature, decadent characters: a dark malty note with hazelnuts and toasted oak, honey, beeswax, tangerines and plums sitting on a bed of delicate peat and just a touch of dark chocolate on the tail.

Glenfarclas distillery

Marypark, Ballindalloch, Banffshire

Tel: +44(0)1807 500209, www.glenfarclas.co.uk

Privately owned by the Grant family since 1836 and with the largest stills in Speyside, Glenfarclas has always produced outstanding whiskies. All of the distillery's output is now filled into sherry casks. You can now buy bottles from every vintage stretching back to 1952 in a series of bottlings known as "The Family Casks."

» Glenfarclas 21 Years Old

This is John Grant's, the Chairman, favorite: aromas of orange marmalade, sweet vanilla, raisins, apples and a little mint mingle together, while the flavor is luscious and big-bodied with gently chewy tannins and plum, coffee and sweet toffee characters finishing with a softly smoky nuttiness.

» Glenfarclas 40 Years Old

EXPERT *Essential* Possibly one of the finest commercially available whiskies. Rich and quite buttery with a little honey, clove and dried apricots supported by leather and good background peat, its flavor is medium sweet, quite malty and mature with touches of chocolate, orange and spice, and the surprisingly fresh finish of malt, licorice and sweet oak lasts forever.

Glenfiddich distillery

Dufftown, Banffshire

Tel: +44(0)1340 820373, www.glenfiddich.com

Another privately owned distillery and owned by another Grant family. Arguably the first widely available single malt as the company was one of the first to actively market its brand, and now the most successful single malt. Demand for the whisky means that the distillery's stillhouse now boasts no fewer than 28 stills. The distillery's visitor center is the most successful in the industry and attracts in excess of 125,000 visitors every year.

» Glenfiddich 30 Years Old

EXPERT *Essential* Not the oldest 'Fiddich, but arguably the best value. Sweet and showing beeswax, a sherry nuttiness, creamy chocolate, and just a suggestion of ginger on the nose, the palate adds cocoa, juicy Satsuma oranges, and pears and finishes with a flourish of apples, coffee, and dark chocolate.

» Why single malts?

Single malts offer consumers a great range of options
and full flavors. Each one is unique to where it comes
from. Each distillery produces a different flavored
spirit, and each single malt is a result of nature rather
than nurture. This has been a contentious point over
recent years, but until someone produces a typical
Ardbeg from Deanston distillery, for example, I will
contend that nature rules.

The accepted understanding is that between 60
and 70 percent of the flavor comes from the cask: the
way that ambient characters interact with the spirit
while it is in the cask; the flavors inherent in the
wood leaching into the spirit during maturation; the
spirit oxidizing over the period; and the manner in
which unwanted flavor characteristics evaporate
through the oak.

Glen Grant distillery

Rothes, Moray

Tel: +44(0)1340 823103, www.glengrant.com

Glen Grant is the world's number-two malt whisky brand and the top-selling whisky in Italy. The distillery dates back to 1840 and, unusually, all the stills are direct fired. To the rear of the distillery is an award-winning garden and, hidden in a safe built into the rock at the top of the garden, there is a secret supply of whisky to refresh you after your climb up the path.

» **Glen Grant 16 Years Old**
Full-bodied, quite austere with fruity apples and apricots supported by soft oaky vanilla and a delicate touch of smokiness, finishing firm and rich with honey and toffee apples.

The Glenlivet distillery

Balindalloch, Banffshire

Tel: +44(0)1542 783220, www.theglenlivet.com

George Gow of The Glenlivet was Scotland's first distiller to take out a license to distill under the 1823 Act. As a result of Royal patronage in 1821, Glenlivet whisky attained a cult status and resulted in the name, Glenlivet, being appended to many distilleries' names. This, the original, has adopted the definitive article to separate its whisky from its imitators.

» **The Glenlivet Archive 21 Years Old**
Citrus, honey, and mature characters such as marmalade, dried apricots and raisins, coconut, and

mahogany are to the fore with beeswax, gently chewy oak tannins, butterscotch, and ginger on the palate; this finishes gloriously complex and surprisingly fresh.

Glenrothes distillery

Rothes, Moray

Tel: +44(0)1340 831248,
www.theglenrothes.com/uk

The distillery pioneered the use of vintages instead of an age statement on its labels, and you will find the difference between a hot vintage like 1993

The morning dram

Whisky has been credited with medicinal properties and, while that claim is regularly disputed, its benefit as personal central heating has been enjoyed for centuries. Dr. Samuel Johnson, in his *A Journey to the Western Isles of Scotland* (1775), recorded "A man of the Hebrides, as soon as he appears in the morning, swallows a glass of whisky; yet they are not a drunken race, at least I never was present at much intemperance; but no man is so abstemious as to refuse the morning dram, which they call a 'skalk.'" Skalk is the anglicization of the Gaelic world "Scailg." Unfortunately, this habit of the morning dram has all but died out.

and a cooler one like 1998 very enlightening. Its make) the spirit it produces) has long been considered as "top dressing" by whisky blenders.

>> **The Glenrothes 1998**

Medium-bodied and sherried with nuts, beeswax, cinnamon, fat, unctuous, creamy hazelnuts, and smoky tangerines; the flavor is round, smooth, creamy, medium-sweet, and rich with dark orange and apricot notes finishing long, softly tangy with a coffee and fruitcake character and quite zesty citrus on the tail.

>> **The Glenrothes 1994**

 Quite full-bodied and fresh, some coffee, vanilla, and honey; with water bringing out cloves, licorice, pears, and ripe peaches, while the palate is rich, nutty, and medium-sweet with a little touch of spice, good weight, some honey, and tangy vanilla; finishing elegant and fresh with some butterscotch and rich lemon curd.

Linkwood distillery

Elgin, Moray

Tel: +44(0)1343 547004

There is a belief among distillers that nothing about a distillery should be

changed in case it changes the character of the spirit. Roderick Mackenzie, who was manager here from 1945 to 1963, didn't even allow the removal of spiders' webs. Despite this, Linkwood, which was originally built in 1821, has been totally rebuilt three times as demand has grown for its make.

» **Linkwood 12 Years Old**
Beautifully apple-scented with some blossom and a soft smokiness at the back; lemon zest plays across the top aroma notes and the flavor is medium-sweet and rounded with apple to the fore and a little smoke, finishing elegantly with some spice and lingering sweetness.

Longmorn distillery

Nr. Elgin, Moray

Tel: +44(0)1542 783400,
www.longmornbrothers.com

Another distillery whose make is under-rated by drinkers but valued as top dressing by blenders. The name comes from the Gaelic "Llanmorgund." which translates as "place of the holy man." as the distillery was built on the site of an ancient church.

» **Longmorn 16 Years Old**
Rich and full-bodied with a cooked apples/grapey fruitiness underlaid by sweet coconut and a hint of pepper, this is medium-sweet and round with flavors of biscuit marzipan, gentle tannins, and a delicate edge of peat. The finish is rich and elegant with a light hint of smokiness.

Macallan distillery

Craigellachie, Moray

Tel: +44(0)1340 871471, www.themacallan.com

Probably the most collected of all malts, there are now quite a formidable range of ages and vintages available in bottle. Established at Easter Elchies farm, close to a fording point on the River Spey, the

036

UNIQUE » RARE » LITTLE-KNOWN » **ULTIMATE EXPERT**

Rosebank No More Established in Falkirk in 1840, for 50 years Rosebank's triple-distilled whisky was in such demand that its customers were put on allocation. But during the first half of the 20th century things changed: owners D.C.L. (Distillers Company Limited) shifted the focus of their business to producing blended whiskies, and Rosebank saw its popularity begin a slow but steady decline.

The staff of the distillery's licensee company, The Distillers Agency Ltd., made strenuous efforts to have the brand promoted in the early 1980s but to no avail. By then, D.C.L. had decided that Cardhu was the only group single malt to be promoted. Rosebank distillery closed in May, 1993.

A very small number of bottlings remain available, such as the fresh, honeyed, herbal, and warmly spiced 1990 Old Malt Cask, but the prices are rising as stocks dwindle.

whisky distilled at the old farm distillery was a popular bonus for the drovers moving their cattle to market. The whisky is known as "The Macallan" and much of the make is aged in sherry casks.

» The Macallan Sherry Oak 12 Years Old

Quite a step up from the 10 Years Old, this has an intensely fruity nose, with peach, apple, banana, black cherry, raspberry, and blackcurrant vying with cinnamon for the top spot. The flavor is more dried fruits—apricots, raisins, and dates in an iced cake—finishing long, rich, and elegant with some cloves coming to the surface.

Speyside distillery

Kingussie, Inverness-shire

Tel: +44(0)1540 661060,
www.speysidedistillery.co.uk

To the east of Kingussie is this relatively new distillery, which had a 34-year gestation period before the spirit first ran on December 12, 1990.

» Speyside 12 Years Old

Quite big-bodied with slightly perfumed dark peat and chocolate notes tinged with medicinal aniseed. The flavor is round and smooth with some beeswax, tar, and toffee, which finishes with a surprisingly delicate peat note.

Highland

The Highland whiskies are drier than Speysides and have more body than those from the Lowlands.

Aberfeldy distillery

Aberfeldy, Perthshire

Tel: +44(0)1887 820330

The distillery building has a definite Presbyterian architectural appearance. Owned by Dewar's and adding its own impact to that blend, the distillery visitor center, Dewar's World of Whisky, has won many awards.

>> **Aberfeldy 18 Years Old**
Quite full-bodied, with waxy notes of heather honey, ripe, mature orange marmalade, lanolin, licorice, and a floral touch; the flavor is sweet, of good body with quite soft peat notes and citrus, ripe orange/lemon, and creamy vanilla, finishing long, very clean, impressive, and ethereal with a note of dry tannin on the end.

Ardmore distillery

Kennethmont, Aberdeenshire

Tel: +44(0)1464 831213, www.ardmorewhisky.com

The distillery's make is a key ingredient in the Teacher's Highland Cream blend. Despite many innovations, the stills remained coal-fired until 2001 when, after a major fire in the stillhouse, they switched to indirect steam heating.

» Ardmore Traditional

Double matured—firstly in bourbon casks and then finished off in small quarter casks, which allow more oak influence. Quite full-bodied and obviously peaty with some creaminess and buttery vanilla backed up by banana, citrus, and a little coconut; the flavor is quite sweet, which you might find jars a little with the earthy peat note; it finishes long with a dark peat note and some butterscotch-coated lemon zest.

Balblair distillery

Edderton, Ross-shire

Tel: +44(0)1862 821273, www.balblair.com

The local area was historically so famous for illicit stills that it has long been known as "The Parish of Peats." There are records of brewing of ale on the site from 1749, although the present distillery was built in 1872.

» Balblair 1989

Medium-sweet, very fresh, and quite full-bodied, this has peach and apple fruit notes with soft, round, toffee vanilla, and delicate peat that resurrects as tarry rope in the dark and tangy finish.

Ben Nevis distillery

Lochy Bridge, Fort William, Inverness-shire

Tel: +44(0)1397 702476,
www.bennevisdistillery.com

Located at the foot of—and taking its name from—Scotland's highest mountain, the distillery was founded by "Long John" MacDonald in 1825. It is now owned by Japanese company, Nikka.

Ben Nevis 1975 26 Years Old

EXPERT *Essential* Quite full-bodied and complex with burnt, treacly toffee, marmalade, oranges, oily, oaky vanilla, and quite a solid peat note; the flavor is full, fruity, chocolate-coated orange, and smoky turkish delight chocolate; finishing long with a dark chocolate note, very elegant, lingering, and complex.

Clynelish distillery

Brora, Sutherland

Tel: +44(0)1408 621444, www.discovering-distilleries.com/clynelish/

The current distillery was built in 1967 next to the original Clynelish, which was established in 1819. The original distillery was set up to utilize the barley grown on the coastal strip by farmers who had been cleared off their property to make way for sheep.

Clynelish 14 Years Old

Quite big-bodied with a citrus fruitiness, a soft malty touch, Demerara sugar-coated soft, sweet oak and chocolate, and cocoa; the flavor is of ripe hazelnuts in creamy vanilla with a dark, oaty peat note; finishing long and elegant with a touch of bitter whole-nut chocolate and tinged with seaweed.

Dalmore distillery

Alness, Ross-shire

Tel: +44(0)1349 882362, www.thedalmore.com

Situated on a very picturesque site on the shores of the Cromarty Firth, Dalmore was established in

1839 by Alexander Matheson, one of the original partners in the international trading company Jardine Matheson. The top half of each spirit still is surrounded by a copper tulip-shaped cooling jacket that contains tubes through which cold water flows. This serves as an additional condenser, ensuring that only the finest alcohols are permitted into the final spirit.

» Dalmore 12 Years Old

Fresh, clean, and medium-dry with good richness, soft vanilla and grapey mandarin orange scents; the flavor has a solid, masculine note supported by elegantly knit peat. The finish is almost dry, lightly malty, and very distinguished.

» Dalmore 40 Years Old

EXPERT *Essential* A whisky that is big and dark, exhibiting brown sugar, medicinal tar, and honey with mature marmalade, tangerines, and delicate peat; the flavor is big, round, medium-sweet, and velvety smooth with spice tingling across your tongue and a very gently chewy toffee note; finishing very long, elegant, and ethereal with a soft peat note.

Edradour distillery

Pitlochry, Perthshire

Tel: +44(0)1796 472095, www.edradour.co.uk

Edradour is the smallest distillery in Scotland, whose output is only enough spirit to fill 12 casks every week. It returned to independent ownership in 2002, when it was taken over by Signatory Vintage Malt Whisky Co. Ltd. The distillery's appearance is similar to Perthshire's farm distilleries of 200 years ago, a collection of farm buildings beside a fast-flowing stream.

» ### Edradour Super Tuscan Finish

EXPERT *Essential* Medium-bodied, grappa-like, and slightly unctuous with notes of chocolate-dipped cherries, forest fruits, and olives; the flavor is medium-sweet and very complex with vanilla custard, dark fruit, chocolate, and spice tingling across the tongue, and then finishing with a flavor of delicate strawberry fruit and a little floral note.

Glendronach distillery

Forgue, By Huntly, Aberdeenshire

www.glendronachdistillery.co.uk

A variety of owners over the years have developed the distillery. Since 1960, it has been an ingredient in the Teacher's Highland Cream blend and was taken over by a group of private investors in 2008. Its make has long been a favorite among whisky aficionados.

» The Glendronach Revival 15 Years Old

EXPERT *Essential* A gentle giant of a whisky that terrifies initially and then shows its compassionate center: quite big-bodied with some candle wax and dried fruit—almost burnt fruit cake, some charred oak, some stewed apples, and a little diesel note; the flavor is full-bodied with a dark peat note, gently chewy with characters of brazil nuts; finishing very long, powerful, and really quite elegant and complex with soft, malty fruit on the tail.

Glenglassaugh distillery

Nr. Portsoy, Banffshire

Tel: +44(0)1261 842367, www.glenglassaugh.com

A distillery that has been mothballed for a total of 70 years in its 135-year history. Despite the fact that Glenglassaugh had been open for less than 10 years when Alfred Barnard visited in 1885, he described its make as "steadily gaining favor in the market" and, despite its many years of closure, its make has continued to be held in high esteem by blenders and consumers. All their whiskies are bottled on site.

Glenglassaugh 26 Years Old

Rich, sherry complexity with buttery vanilla shortbread notes dipped in strawberries and creamy toffee; the flavor is medium-dry and nutty with licorice, almonds, and dried fruits; finishing fresh, slightly minty, and sherried.

Glengoyne distillery

Dumgoyne, Killearn, Stirlingshire

Tel: +44(0)1360 550254, www.glengoyne.com

Nestling under Dumgoyne Hill, the distillery has been fiercely independent of the large distillers

The Keepers of the Quaich

In 1988, The Keepers of the Quaich was formed at Blair Castle in Perthshire, founded by a group of competing distilling companies to promote Scotch whisky and encourage other companies within the industry. A quaich is a communal drinking bowl that originated in 17th-century Edinburgh and Glasgow. The society's quaich is 24 inches in diameter and was created by Graham Stewart, a silversmith from Dunblane. Membership is by invitation only and The Keepers are individuals who have made some significant contribution to the industry. Their motto reads "Uisgebeatha Gu Brath," which, translated from the Gaelic, means "Whisky Forever"!

during its 177 years. The distillery's warehouses are south of the Highland Line, which takes the form of the A81 road as it passes the distillery, which sits on the other, Highland, side of the road.

» Glengoyne 40 Years Old

Medium-bodied, with some greenery aromas, Demerara sugar and red-skinned apples; spice notes open up of nutmeg, fennel, and dark, nutty toffee. The flavor is medium-dry, with soft, rich toffee, good body, and a cereal note. It has a smooth, unctuous, oily vanilla character, with some honeycomb, and finishes very long, clean, and ethereal with some cardamom and a note that is almost grapefruit. It is complex with a richness that lasts and a dark, drying finish.

Glenmorangie distillery

Tain, Ross-shire

Tel: +44(0)1862 892477, www.glenmorangie.com

One of the leading malts around the world, it has the tallest stills in Scotland, at just under 17 feet. The height of the stills means that only the finest and most delicate of flavors fall over the lyne arm, which runs from the head of the still to the condenser. As of spring 2009, the number of stills increased to 12. The company has been very innovative in its packaging and, in many cases, has done away with age statements on its bottles.

» Glenmorangie 25 Years Old

Quite big-bodied and pungent, intense, musky, and perfumed with a homemade blackcurrant jam aroma backed up by sandalwood, vanilla, some spice, and a hint of dark chocolate; the flavor is quite big-bodied, with notes of cocoa and chocolate, spice and luscious ripe orange; finishing round and with a note of creamy macchiato, some dried orange peel and yet retaining a mouthwatering zingy, citrus zestiness.

Pulteney distillery

Wick, Caithness

Tel: +44(0)1955 602371, www.oldpulteney.com

The most northerly distillery on the UK mainland and named after Pulteneytown, the district of the town of Wick in which the distillery was built. Wick was built on the fishing industry, but it is distilling which has survived as the fishing industry became a pale shadow of what it once was. The distillery's wash stills are truncated, with the lyne arms coming off below the top of the stills. When the stills were delivered, it was discovered that they were too tall for the stillhouse, so the tops were cut off. The result is that the heavier alcohols do not fall over the lyne arm, making the spirit more elegant.

» **Old Pulteney 17 Years Old**

 Medium-bodied, slightly vegetal and

nutty with notes of coconut and pineapple supported by tarry rope and a soft sea influence; the flavor is medium-dry, of good weight, rich, soft, and easy with a touch of spice and some malty honey; finishing long and elegant with licorice, pine needles, and salty lips.

Tullibardine distillery

Blackford, Perthshire

Tel: +44(0)1764 682252, www.tullibardine.com

The work of leading distillery designer William Delmé-Evans and built in 1949, the buildings of this distillery had lain mothballed for 10 years when they were bought by a quartet of businessmen who have developed the site as an essential tourist destination. The area is known for the quality of its water: a brewery on the site was awarded a Royal Charter following a visit from King James IV in 1488 and there are two mineral-water companies based within 5 miles of the distillery.

» **Tullibardine 1993**
Fresh and malty with a peppery peat note, an edge of sweetness, and a green, hedgerow character; the flavor is medium-dry with good body and a character of creamy hazelnut caramels; finishing long, rich, and elegant with the malt springing up again on the tail.

Lowland

Lowland whiskies are the lightest and driest of Scotland's output and are located in an area south of a line drawn between Cardross in the west and Dundee in the east.

Auchentoshan distillery

Dalmuir, Clydebank, Dunbartonshire

Tel: +44(0)1389 878561, www.auchentoshan.co.uk

Auchentoshan is being styled as "Glasgow's Malt Whisky" as it is produced within the boundaries of the greater city. Triple-distilled and unpeated, its production has long reflected its agricultural origins, with the name being derived from the Gaelic for "corner of the field."

» Auchentoshan 12 Years Old

Fresh and clean with floral and toasty toffee notes and some creamy, buttery aromas; the flavors are dry and rich with limey citrus and peach; finishing with a touch of cereal and some perfume on the tail.

Bladnoch distillery

Bladnoch, Wigtown, Dumfries & Galloway

Tel: +44(0)1988 402235, www.bladnoch.co.uk

Originally founded in 1817 and owned by Irish distillers Dunville's for many years, it is once again in Irish hands, having been sold to Raymond Armstrong, who recommenced distilling in November 2000. Bladnoch is the most southerly distillery in Scotland and home to the Whisky School, where students can get a hands-on three-day experience of making whisky.

» **Bladnoch 8 Years Old**

EXPERT *Essential* A great, zingily fresh lunchtime malt, full of life, medium-bodied and malty, showing zesty lemons and grapefruit, a slight medicinal note, some cereal, hazelnut, and toffee/vanilla; the flavors are medium-dry and rich with an oily, unctuous vanilla smoothness; finishing soft, languorous, and lazily decadent.

Islay

Islay's whiskies are the most peat- and sea-influenced of all Scotland's malts. The smoky character is one you either love or hate; very few of you will sit on this fence. The island is only 14 miles long and 8 miles wide and the Atlantic Ocean weather washes over the island, greatly influencing its whiskies.

Ardbeg distillery

near Port Ellen, Isle of Islay

Tel: +44(0)1496 302244, www.ardbeg.com

Ardbeg's make is the most heavily peated of all Scotland's whiskies, at 50 parts per million. Its make has always been a favorite of Islay aficionados, but it was closed more often than it was open in the 30 years prior to being taken over by Glenmorangie in 1997.

» Ardbeg Corryvreckan

EXPERT *Essential* With everything that the 10 Years Old has—but in spades! Tar, chocolate, and burnt mahogany, notes of shellfish, citrus—orange leaps out—backed up by sandalwood; the flavor is dry, big-bodied, and intensely smokily Ardbeg, showing smoked fish and spice; finishing long, intense, and explosive with huge peat notes and lemon and lime on the tail.

Bowmore distillery

Bowmore, Isle of Islay

Tel: +44(0)1496 810671,
www.bowmore.com

The distillery stands fortress-like, alongside the harbour in the town of Bowmore. The distillery gave a warehouse to the town and this was converted to a swimming pool, which is heated by the waste heat from the distillery. The various bottlings from the company have proved very collectable in recent years.

» Bowmore 18 Years Old

Quite full with damp autumn leaves and chestnuts, charred stick peat and violets; with water, heather opens up with some green-apple skins, caramel, tobacco, and seaweed. It has good body and the flavor is round and sherried with licorice, floral, and chocolate with a carbolic note; finishing long with a sense of sweetness, quite rich and with a burnt chocolate note on the tail.

Bruichladdich distillery

Bruichladdich, Isle of Islay

Tel: +44(0)1496 950221, www.bruichladdich.com

The lightest and most delicate of Islay's whiskies. In 1995, the distillery was closed and looked as if it was going to be left to rot, but a consortium of 25 private investors took it over in December 2001. Since then there has been a mind-boggling array of bottlings on the shelves. It is the only Islay to be bottled at the distillery after the installation of a bottling line in 2008. Affectionately known as "Laddie." Bruichladdich is pronounced "Brew-ich-laddie."

» **Bruichladdich 15 Years Old**
Medium-bodied with a touch of nuttiness—hazelnuts and peanuts—coated in a rich, malty tablet and some beeswax. The flavor is round, smooth, of medium-body and medium-dry with softly chewy tannins and gently peated; finishing quite ethereal and elegant with a touch of perfume and some peanut.

Caol Ila distillery

Port Askaig, Isle of Islay

Tel: +44(0)1496 840207

On the east coast, just to the north of Port Askaig, the stillhouse has the finest view of any distillery across to the Paps of Jura. Sea water is used in condensing the evaporate from Caol Ila's stills. Caol Ila is pronounced "Kaal-eela."

» Malting and fermentation

Bowmore distillery adds an extra layer of flavor to its whisky by turning to tradition. In exactly the same manner of a farmer of 500 years ago, Bowmore's barley is soaked in the peat-stained waters of the River Laggan and laid out onto its malting floor, encouraging the seeds to germinate. During germination, the starch inside the seed is converted to fermentable sugars. The grain is then heated over a peat-fed open fire whose heat stops the germination so that, while some of the fermentable sugars have been used to fuel growth, there remains a considerable amount within the seed's shell. Once dried, the green malt is ground into a coarse flour known as "grist." To this, hot water is added, giving a hot, sweet, sticky liquid called "wort." Yeast is added to the wort and bacterial fermentation converts the sugar to alcohol, resulting in a high-alcohol beer known as "wash."

Caol Ila 18 Years Old

 Big-bodied and powerful with a classic Caol Ila nose of burnt heather roots complemented by soft oaky vanilla. There is also a touch of antiseptic and some citrus. The flavor is dry and powerful, rich, smooth, and charred with a slight edge of sweetness, which finishes with notes of tar and chocolate, dry smoke and melon.

Laphroaig distillery

Nr. Port Ellen, Isle of Islay

Tel: +44(0)1496 302418,
www.laphroaig.com

Situated on the south coast of Islay and facing the prevailing south-westerly weather, Laphroaig's annual storm-damage bill is considerable; in high winds, the seaweed is piled up against the distillery walls and can often be found hanging from the roof. This is why Laphroaig's make is so sea-tainted.

Laphroaig 18 Years Old

Quite soft for Laphroaig, honey, creamy toffee apples, and pepper supported by sooty peat smoke and some tar with seaweed, iodine, and ginger. The flavor is big-bodied, dry, and of peat smoke with a sweetness, tarry oranges, and honeyed seaweed; finishing spicy with sweetly toasted oak and a bonfire on the beach.

Campbeltown

In the early 20th century, Campbeltown was known as the "whisky capital" of Scotland because of the number of distilleries—at one point, there were 32 in production. Over-production during Prohibition in the USA led to a reduction in quality, and consumers lost faith in Campbeltown's whiskies. By 1935, all the distilleries had closed. Since then, only three have reopened, Glen Scotia, Glengyle, and Springbank.

Springbank distillery

Longrow, Campbeltown, Argyll

Tel: +44(0)1586 552085,
www.springbankwhisky.com

The team at Springbank could be called "eccentric": they do things their way. It has been run by members of the same family for 173 years. Everything, from malting through to bottling and despatch, is carried out at this site. Although the stillhouse has three stills, it is not triple-distilled; it is distilled two and a half times. Longrow (heavily peated) and Hazelburn (triple-distilled) are also produced at Springbank.

» Springbank 18 Years Old

EXPERT
Essential
Of medium weight with rich, oily oak and marzipan, quite a lot of red fruit—strawberries and raspberries—supported by licorice and dark honey and treacle toffee; the flavor has dried fruits: apricots, raisins, pineapple, and coconut; finishing with great length, some smoky oak, dark chocolate, a little tarry rope, licorice, and Springbank's classic salty lips.

Other Islands

Highland Park distillery

Holm Road, Kirkwall, Orkney

Tel: +44(0) 1856 873107, www.highlandpark.co.uk

Scotland's most northerly distillery is located on Orkney's Mainland. Twenty percent of the distillery's malt requirements are still produced from its malting floor. Orkney's cool climatic conditions—the average temperature in winter is 43°F and 59°F in summer—mean that the whisky matures slowly and evenly.

» ### Highland Park 40 Years Old

EXPERT *Essential* Quite full-bodied and mature with notes of oranges, vanilla, honey, and eucalyptus—soft, buttery, and creamy with notes of hazelnut, brioche, and popcorn. The flavor is medium-dry, round, and rich, a touch of spice tingles across the tongue; there are hints of orange, walnuts, and pistachios, buttered whole-wheat bread and it is smooth and creamy. The finish has a long and ethereal center with rich edges, a little tangy note, and some salt appears on the tail.

Isle of Arran distillery

Lochranza, Isle of Arran

Tel: +44(0)1770 830264, www.arranwhisky.com

Legal distilling was reestablished on the island of Arran after 150 years. The modern distillery is traditional in its outlook but blends easily within the surrounding landscape. Golden eagles inhabit the hills above the distillery and are a frequent feature of the distillery's open days.

>> **Arran Rowan Tree**
A more delicate style, with floral, toffee, biscuity, and lavender notes, a hint of coffee and some citrus— orange and lime; the flavor is drier than the core malts, clean, rich, and smooth with a wee touch of spice, and some chocolate-topped cappuccino; finishing long, clean, fresh, and quite ethereal with a touch of espresso and a lavender floral note.

Isle of Jura distillery

Craighouse, Isle of Jura

Tel: +44(0)1496 820240, www.isleofjura.com

Closed in the early 1900s following an argument over rent, the distillery was rebuilt by William Delmé-Evans and finally produced again in 1963. As the crow flies, Craighouse is 66 miles from the company's head office in Glasgow, but the journey by road takes almost a whole day, covers 130 miles by road, and includes two ferry trips.

>> **Jura Superstition**
Big-bodied and rich with a dried fruit note, rich nuttiness, toffee, marzipan, heather honey, and lots of earthy peat; the flavor is quite big-bodied, medium-dry, but very rich and smooth with honey and a creaminess supported by solid, approachable peat. The finish is long, complex, and impressively rich with a sweet edge, some licorice, and ocean-breeze notes with a touch of pine needles.

Blends

The blending of heavily flavored malts with more refined grain whiskies gives the public a more easy-drinking whisky with some elegance.

» **Black Bull 12 Years Old (Duncan Taylor & Co.)**
Weighty, chocolate-coated, sherried green apples and peaches with quite delicate peat; smooth and elegant.

» **Black Bottle (Burn Stewart)**
EXPERT *Essential* Superbly blended, solid, of good weight with burnt heather roots and chocolate with sea notes and a hint of sweetness.

» **Chivas Regal 12 Years Old (Pernod Ricard)**
Smooth and sweet, honeyed, fruity, and gently nutty; a great blend with complex undertones.

» **Cutty Sark (Edrington)**
Fresh and honeyed with vanilla oak and orange/citrus—a wonderful lunchtime drink.

» **Dewar's (Bacardi)**
Honey, vanilla, soft peat smoke, toffee, and tablet with a firm note of malt; wonderful balance, elegant and easy.

» **Monkey Shoulder (William Grant)**
EXPERT *Essential* A blend of three Speyside malts, quite full-bodied, grapefruit- and pineapple-flavored with spice, chocolate, and toffee.

» Irish whiskey

Irish distilleries

The Irish arguably were the first people to make whiskey. Its origins can be traced back to the 6th century AD, and Sir Walter Raleigh dropped by to pick up a cask of Irish whiskey from Cork in 1595 when he was en route to Guyana.

Scotch and Irish whiskies

The main difference between Scotch and Irish whiskey is that the latter is lighter because the Irish use a large portion of unmalted barley in their pot still production.

The malt for Scotch whisky is dried over an open peat fire, which means the smoke permeates the grains and this smoky taste carries right through to the final whisky. By contrast, in Ireland, the malt is dried in closed kilns so that only hot air dries the grains, not smoke. Few Irish whiskeys in recent years have used peat for the drying of their green malt; they have had plentiful supplies of coal. By installing a number of different still shapes and sizes in their stillhouses, the Irish are able to produce a wide variety of differently flavored spirits within the same distillery.

The art of the distiller is to separate and retain the good elements of the alcohol family—the ones that, when mature, will make a good whiskey—and to separate and discard the undesirable elements—the ones that will simply give a hangover. In Ireland, this is done by distilling three times. The triple distillation produces a more refined, less characterful spirit than double distillation.

Diminishing distilleries

It is estimated that, at the start of the 18th century, there were around 2,000 distilleries in Ireland, but when the Irish Distillers Group was formed in 1966, there were only five distilleries left in production. Shortly afterwards, Jameson & Powers in Dublin, Tullamore, and Cork distilleries ceased distilling. This reduced Ireland's distilleries to two: Bushmills in the north and the "new" Midleton in the south. Since then, Cooley's has opened up and there is currently talk of a distillery being developed on the Dingle Peninsula in the southwest.

The continuous still

When Aeneas Coffey filed his patent for his continuous still in 1830, he was the proprietor of the Dock distillery in Dublin, which may have been why he was unable to get any of his fellow Irish distillers to use his newly invented still. They insisted on sticking with their pot stills, which were more expensive to run and produced a more characterful spirit. Instead, he went to Scotland, where he was welcomed with open arms by the Steins and Haigs, who adopted the continuous still and developed grain whiskey and, in the fullness of time, allowed the development of blended whiskey.

Pure pot still

Old Bushmills distillery

Bushmills, County Antrim, Northern Ireland

Tel: +44(0)282 0731521, www.bushmills.com

The world's original licensed distillery, with an original license date of 1608, although there are records of distillation in the area as far back as 1276. The stillhouse contains 10 stills, which are able to conjure up a wide variety of whiskey flavors.

» ### Bushmills 16 Years Old

EXPERT *Essential* Full-bodied, fresh, and slightly green with a gooseberry character. It has a rich, woody nuttiness and is medium-sweet with a toffee character; the flavor is almost dry with good body, smooth, dark; finishing with a good richness, a dark complexity, and an almost mahogany-flavored chewiness.

Cooley distillery

Riverstown, Dundalk, County Louth, Ireland

Tel: +353(0)429 37610, www.cooleywhiskey.com

Cooley's was established in 1989 with one still just south of the border with the North. The company's creation broke the dominance of the industry by Irish Distillers, and its presence enlivened the category. Fiercely independent and innovative, Colley has reintroduced peat flavors into Irish whiskey with its Connemara brand.

» **Tyrconnel**

Fresh and clean with a touch of licorice, a good, ripe richness, medium-sweet and quite round with a slight unctuous character; the flavor is medium-sweet, fresh, round, and smooth with quite good body; finishing clean with honey and an almost barley sugar sweetness and a slight citrus note.

» **Connemara**

Quite full-bodied, fresh, and medium-dry with a round fruitiness and a good measure of slightly green peatiness; the flavor is medium-sweet, with good body, a nice weight of peat and a round, dark nuttiness. It finishes long and clean with a good background smokiness.

» **Greenore Single Grain**

Light, delicate, fresh with sweet bourbon, oaky, vanilla notes and peaches; the flavor is rich and soft, quite mouth-watering with an oily oak/barley sugar character, that finishes fresh, clean, and crisp.

Midleton distillery

Midleton, County Cork, Ireland

Tel: +353(0)214 613594

Built alongside the original Midleton distillery, which now forms the distillery's visitor center, in 1975, the new distillery is hidden from the public's eyes and yet produces most of the Irish whiskeys you will see on bar rails around the world. It has three

In the details

The science of selecting and mixing grain for spirit

» Barley beginnings

It is essential to have quality grains—you can make poor spirit from good grains, but you cannot make good spirit from poor-quality grains.

Among the important factors that allow a distillery to produce a unique spirit is the mix of cereals used at the brewing stage of the process, in particular the ratio of malted barley to unmalted barley, which is of prime importance. Unmalted barley was originally used because the Malt Act of 1725 taxed malted barley. Nowadays, each of the Irish Distillers' brands has a different mix of malted and unmalted barley, and this mix is very important to the final flavor profile of each whiskey.

There is a traditional test used to determine the best barley, which is to take a well-filled barley grain and cut it in two. A white color means that it's suitable for milling and conversion. This simple test is as relevant today as it was many years ago.

column stills as well as nine very large pots. Outside the visitor center is the world's largest pot still (31,648 gallons or 143,874 liters), which used to be worked inside the old distillery and is so large that they had to install it and build the distillery around it before supporting it from the roof to stop it imploding.

» **Midleton Very Rare 2010**

EXPERT *Essential* Medium-bodied, lemon-scented with notes of honey, malt, charred mahogany, tea, zesty grapefruit, and blackcurrant; the flavors are balanced, rich and dry with a touch of spice, some mint and some nutty toffee. The finish is long, complex, and sweet with syrup and menthol occurring.

Blended Irish whiskeys

Because Irish malts have not developed in the same way that Scotch malts have, you will not find many on shelves around the world, but the industry has quite successfully developed the blended trade. And now, the blends are what Ireland is most famous for. Their capacity for producing two different flavors within the same stillhouse (one flavor produced, for example, by combining the effects of a big fat still with two small thin stills, the other by combining a tall, bulbous still with a small thin one and a big fat one) has imbued them with a flexibility to be envied by other areas of the whiskey world.

» Black Bush (Bushmills)

A blend from Bushmills distillery with a relatively high (70 percent or more) malt content and aged for longer than average, predominantly in sherry cask. This has a sweet, rich, and sherried nose with fresh, malty, fudge and toffee flavor with a little crisp gooseberry fruit; finishing with some chocolate.

» Bushmills White Label (Midleton)

Also known as "White Bush," this is a blend of malt whiskey from the distillery of the same name and grain whiskey from Midleton. It is malty with some oaky vanilla and honey and a floral touch; the flavor is clean, medium-dry, and simple with some elderflower finishing with a spicy note.

» Coleraine (Pernod Ricard)

Oak aroma characters—leather, caramel, and beeswax—with medium-sweet flavors of melon and vanilla caramel; finishing quite dry with some easy spice.

» Clontarf Classic (Clontarf Distilling Company)

Medium-bodied with a touch of smoke, some orange, and spirity toffee; the flavor is medium-bodied and medium-sweet with butterscotch and toffee underpinned by a light touch of smoke, and it finishes sweet with just a touch of spice.

>> **Crested Ten (Pernod Ricard)**
Big and impressive with hazelnutty sherry notes and ginger; the flavor is smooth with honey, toffee, and chocolate; finishing dry, clean, and with the sherry nuttiness reprising.

>> **Green Spot (Pernod Ricard)**
EXPERT *Essential* Medium-bodied and fresh with new-mown grass, mint, honey, and cocoa notes; it is mouth-wateringly zingily fresh and clean, with rich heather honey and spice finishing long, elegant and hedgerow leafy with an espresso note.

>> **Jameson's 12 Years Old (Pernod Ricard)**
The sherry cask influence is instantly noticeable, nutty, raisined, and sweet, then the whiskey takes over with crisp apple dipped in honey and coated in vanilla.

>> **Kilbeggan Blend (Cooley)**
Zingily clean and citrusy lime and some apple on the nose, with medium-sweet, smooth toasted malt and some honey on the palate, which finishes rich with a fresh greenness and some spicy oak.

>> **Locke's (Cooley)**
Big and fruity—apples, oranges, and lemons—with some mint, the flavors are rounded and sweet with unctuous oak and spearmint, and finishes with some chocolate.

>> **Murphy's (Pernod Ricard)**
Quite light with toffee/fudge and some varnish with a hint of peanut butter; the flavor is grassy and

Words from the wise

Jeff Arnett Master distiller,
Jack Daniels, USA

» On adding ice to whiskey

Some people frown on putting ice or water into whiskey, which I think is a mistake. It's all a matter of personal taste, circumstance, and the type of whiskey.

I drink Jack Daniels' Single Barrel, on the rocks. This is a travesty according to some drinkers from the world's cooler countries, as they claim that the addition of ice kills the flavor. I agree that too much ice can dull the whiskey's more subtle flavors, but that doesn't mean you can't add any.

Tennessee's climate is too hot to not add ice—our summer temperatures are regularly in excess of 80°F and often remain at that level for several weeks on end—so I drink it on the rocks to cool me down. In the winter it gets cold, so I drink it neat when I need warming up. At the end of the day, the final choice of how you drink it is up to you; your palate dictates your method of enjoyment. Just go ahead and enjoy it, but remember—in moderation.

gooseberry-fruited, finishing clean and lightly spicy with some soft vanilla.

» Paddy's (Pernod Ricard)

Medium-bodied with floral and apple/peach overtones, its flavor is medium-dry and perfumed with soft, smooth oaky vanilla toffee notes finishing dry and malty.

» Power's (Pernod Ricard)

Clean, fresh, with a little honeyed floral note and crisp, zesty citrus cereals; the flavor is medium-dry and of medium weight with some beeswax and leathery oak; finishing very crisp, fresh dry, and clean.

» Redbreast (Pernod Ricard)

EXPERT *Essential* Honeyed and fruity with intense grapefruit and gooseberry notes, some clean, sherried hazelnuts and rich, creamy fruitcake; the flavor is big-bodied, spicy, gingery, dark, sherried brazil nuts, all swimming in treacle and finishing long and complex with licorice and Chinese spices.

» Tullamore Dew (William Grant)

Grassy and gooseberried with some toasty oak notes; the flavor is medium-bodied, medium-sweet, and fruity with caramel, cinnamon, and some sherry rubber finishing long, sweet, and beeswax-coated.

» American whiskey

Bourbon production

American whiskey reflects the production techniques of Scotland and Ireland because Scottish and Irish settlers, fleeing persecution in their home countries in the 18th century, brought their whiskey-making skills with them to the US. Thus, it was natural that America's indigenous grains should be distilled into American whiskeys.

Variations from other whiskeys

You will find some similarities of flavor to Scotch and Irish whiskeys, but also that the very different climatic conditions in the Americas impose a different character on the spirit. The heat means that long maturation is very unusual in America. Obviously, the different mix of grains has a bearing on the final flavor also. American whiskeys are more robust than their Scottish and Irish counterparts and can assimilate the overpowering influence of new wood, without the whiskeys' flavors being swamped by the oak. If Scotch and Irish whiskeys are matured in new wood, the flavors are completely dominated by the oak's characters.

Classifying a bourbon

Bourbon is a style of whiskey. It need not come from Bourbon County in Kentucky, but can be made in almost any part of the United States. Evan Williams is reputed to have been Kentucky's first commercial distiller when he set up in Louisville distillery in 1783. In 1791, Congress in Washington imposed an excise tax on whiskey, inciting the "Whiskey Rebellion," a part of which was the Boston Tea Party, and leading to the migration of north-eastern distillers into Kentucky.

At one point, there were 2,000 American distilleries producing bourbon; following Prohibition, there are now no more than a dozen in Kentucky.

As a generalization, you will find that bourbon's first distillation takes place in a "beer" still—a continuous still—and the second distillation occurs in a "doubler" still, which is a pot still.

Nowadays, to be called a bourbon, the spirit must:

» be produced in the United States of America
» be produced from a mash bill consisting of at least 51 percent corn
» be distilled to a strength of no more than 160 proof (80 percent a.b.v.)
» be matured in new, charred, white oak barrels at no more than 125 proof (62.5 percent a.b.v.)
» have nothing added to the final product except pure water
» state the duration of its aging on its label, if aged for less than four years.
» if aged for a minimum of two years, it may be called "straight bourbon"
» be bottled at a minimum alcoholic strength of 80 proof (40 percent a.b.v.).

073

Kentucky bourbon

Barton distillery

Bardstown, Kentucky

Tel: 502 348 3991

Originally founded by Tom Moore in 1879, the current distillery was built in 1946. A utilitarian distillery, its fermenters and stills are constructed from stainless steel; the sole condescension to tradition are the doubler still and the tops of the beer stills, which are copper.

» **Kentucky Gentleman**
The nose is a little dumb with some sweet oak and toffee, while the flavor is big and hits the palate

The Father of Bourbon

The practice of charring barrels became established in 1789 when the Rev. Elijah Craig, a Baptist minister and farmer, experienced a fire in the barn where he stored empty whiskey barrels. Craig put his new make into the burned barrels anyway and soon discovered that his whiskey was aging better than it had done in new oak casks. It picked up more color and flavor, and his discovery earned Craig the title of "The Father of Bourbon."

suddenly, opening out to sweet, ripe citrus and cherry fruit backed by some oak and maple syrup. It finishes well, but dry with an oily, oaky, nutty character.

Jim Beam distillery

Clermont, Kentucky

Tel: 502 543 9877, www.jimbeam.com

Originally farmers in Kentucky's bluegrass hills, the Beams began distilling in 1795. They have been using successive strains of the same yeast culture for the past 75 years, and the strain is so jealously protected that samples of it are stored at several different sites. As the world's best-selling bourbon, they filled their 10,000,000th barrel in 2005.

» **Knob Creek**
Rich and ripe, quite intensely sweet aromas of orange marmalade, buttery vanilla with a little almond and a hint of char; the flavor is delicate, but complex with chocolate and spice, apple and some gently chewy, nutty oak; finishing with sticky marshmallows, cocoa, leather, and great length.

Buffalo Trace distillery

Frankfort, Kentucky

Tel: 502 696 5926, www.buffalotrace.com

Buffalo Trace has had many names over the years, from Old Fire Copper, through Old Stagg, Ancient Age, and, finally, Buffalo Trace in 1999, in memory of the huge herds of buffalo that used to cross the Kentucky River close to this point. All their whiskeys are of the small-batch variety.

» Climate control

Most Kentucky whiskeys are aged in rick warehouses up to nine stories high, with barrels stacked three high on each floor. Kentucky has hot summers and cold winters, causing the top floors to bake in the summer heat while the ground floor remains cool, and in winter the top floor retains some heat while the ground is cold. As a result, the whiskey on each floor matures at a different rate: the barrels on the top floor mature faster than those on the bottom.

The Kentuckians have dealt with the problem in several ways. By opening windows they allow air to circulate and dissipate the summer's heat. Some distillers move their barrels between the floors, levelling out the maturation, while others blend whiskeys from each floor to maintain consistency. The premium blends and small-batch bottling come from the middle floors where the temperature fluctuations are less extreme.

George T. Stagg 15 Years Old

 This is the 2009 release of the 15-year-old. The nose is pretty huge and complex: mint, toffee, leather, cinnamon, chocolate, marmalade and maple syrup; the sweet-corn flavor has a good belt of spice with juicy tangerines, cocoa, coffee and finishes with quite an alcoholic burn that seems (strangely) well-balanced with sweet tobacco and toffee-dipped cherries.

Four Roses distillery

Lawrenceburg, Kentucky

Tel: 502 839 3436, www.fourroses.us

The buildings at the distillery are unique in distilling as well as in Kentucky, being built in a Spanish Mission style. The company combines five proprietary yeast strains with two separate mash bills to produce 10 distinct and handcrafted bourbon recipes, each with its own unique character.

» Four Roses Single Barrel

Rich and quite restrained, perfumed, floral, with spice, nutmeg, creamy vanilla toffee, orange and lime; the flavor is smooth, soft and rounded, medium-dry with some sweet mint and buttery, toasted vanilla; finishing gently chewy with a hit of cinnamon and the toast lingering.

Words from the wise

Eric Gregory President, Kentucky Distillers' Association, USA

» Visiting distilleries

When visiting Kentucky, it is best to avoid shut-down season—the hotter months when water supplies have a tendency to dry up and the distilleries to shut down. The length of this season can vary from a few weeks to a few months, depending on the distillery and the reliability of its water source. If you're touring between the Kentucky Derby (May) and the Kentucky Bourbon Festival (September), check with the distillery when planning your trip. Naturally, you should use The Kentucky Bourbon Trail® (www.kybourbontrail.com) to help plan your visit.

The Kentucky Bourbon Festival in the middle of September is great fun. It celebrates everything bourbon, with events at all the distilleries and elsewhere across the state: art, barrel-making demonstrations, hot air balloons, music, food, and, of course, tasting samplers. This is the best time to visit and share bourbon with fellow whiskey lovers.

Heaven Hill distillery

Bardstown, Kentucky

Tel: 502 337 1000, www.heaven-hill.com

In 1935, the Shapira brothers opened Heaven Hill distillery. They filled their 6,000,000th barrel in November 2010. The distillery experienced a huge fire in 1996 that consumed a number of full warehouses and saw an asphalt road melt under the river of burning whiskey. Despite this, the company survived; the warehouses have been rebuilt, stocks have been replaced and sales continue to grow.

» **Elijah Craig 18 Years Old Single Barrel**

EXPERT *Essential* Huge, imposing, complex and intense: custard, bananas, coconut, buttery popcorn and creamy toffee apples; the flavor is medium-sweet and smoky spicy with lemony citrus and gently chewy oaky crème brûlée vanilla; finishing extremely elegant and well-balanced with maple oak and a distinctly smoky tail.

Maker's Mark distillery

Loretto, Kentucky

Tel: 270 865 2099, www.makersmark.com

In 1953, Bill Samuels Sr. bought the Buck's Spring distillery in Happy Hollow. He dropped the rye from his mash bill and substituted wheat: 70 percent corn, 14 percent wheat and 16 percent malted barley, a formula which continues to this day. A small-batch distillery—they were filling 38 barrels a day, while the "big boys" were filling 1,300—when *The New York Times* carried a front-page story in 1980 about

Maker's Mark and all of a sudden everyone wanted to drink it.

» **Maker's Mark**
Soft, sweet, ripe corn and bubblegum; with water, Demerara sugar, honey, shellac varnish, red-skinned apples, and ripe pineapple come out; the flavor is

Parker's Heritage Collection Kentucky's summer heat means that bourbons mature faster than Scotch or Irish whiskeys. This means that it is very unusual for a bourbon to exceed 20 years of age, because after this period the wood characters become too dominant.

Sometimes a barrel or two will surprise the distillers by maturing well and in a balanced manner for as many as 27 years. Naturally, the angels have sipped away at the cask's contents, so the volume of whiskey remaining after this prolonged maturation period is small. The bottled whiskey is expensive to reflect these losses.

Parker's Heritage Collection is an on-going series of very limited releases by Heaven Hill of cask-strength whiskeys solely intended for the US market. With a little effort, you will find the intensely rich, elegant, toffee-dipped summer fruit-flavored Heritage Collection 27 Years Old available (unofficially) in other countries as well.

» Cask creativity

There is a great deal of experimentation going on
with barrels in the whiskey world at the moment,
and it's not just a case of keeping the whiskey in the
cask for a couple of years longer.

Maker's 46 is a prime example. Whiskey maker,
Kevin Smith explained, "We started off trying
smaller barrels; we tried bigger barrels; we tried
cubes; we tried all sorts of things. When the
cooperage offered us the Profile 46 stave (that had
been seared on the outside), it caused the flavors that
we were looking for: the oak-toasted aromas to come
through, those deeper, richer, vanilla/caramel notes.
And the most amazing piece was that the spiciness
that came out of it wasn't bitter. The flavors coming
through are reminiscent of Maker's Mark, but what
we've done is add a little more spice, but no tannins.
None of these changes make it necessarily better; it
is just a slightly different Maker's Mark."

medium-bodied, medium-sweet and rich with a little spicy, oily vanilla and some toffeed red fruits. The finish is long, perfumed, elegant and soft with a touch of maple syrup and butterscotch.

» Maker's 46

EXPERT *Essential* This is a Maker's Mark fully matured for a few months more, in contact with seared French oak staves. Rich, ripe, rounder and more refined than usual Maker's Mark with sweet-corn; water brings out toffee apples, honey, home baking, creamy vanilla and licorice; the flavor is drier than Maker's Mark and it grows in the mouth with gently chewy oak, good body, spice and honey; finishing long, very elegant and ethereal, flowing into tangy spice on the tail.

Wild Turkey distillery

Lawrenceburg, Kentucky

Tel: 502 839 4544, www.wildturkeybourbon.com

Founded as the Ripy Family distillery in 1869, the distillery sits 259 feet above the Kentucky River. It was not until 1940 that the Wild Turkey brand was created after a distillery executive took some of the whiskey on an annual wild turkey shoot. His friends enjoyed it so much that, the following year, they asked him to bring some of that same "Wild

Turkey" bourbon along with him—and the brand was born.

» **Wild Turkey 8 Years Old 101**

EXPERT *Essential* Medium-bodied, quite delicate and subdued with rich, creamy vanilla leather; with water, orange marmalade and baked apples with cinnamon on buttery toast comes out; the flavor is medium-dry, rich and medium-bodied with dry tannins and tingling spice; finishing long, huge, rich, smooth and elegant with creamy oak and sweet-corn, ending dry on the tail. Despite the high strength (50.5 percent a.b.v.), the alcohol is very well integrated into the flavor.

Woodford Reserve distillery

Versailles, Kentucky

Tel: 859 879 1812, www.woodfordreserve.com

Originally called the Oscar Pepper distillery when erected in 1838, it was renamed Woodford Reserve distillery in 1996. It's mash bill is 72 percent corn, 18 percent rye, and 10 percent malted barley. Unusually, Woodford Reserve uses three copper pot stills built by Forsyth's of Rothes in Scotland and its spirit is produced using triple distillation.

» **Woodford Reserve**

EXPERT *Essential* Rich, orange, charred vanilla oak with dark-chocolate-dipped raisins, ginger, and vanilla; the flavor is full of soft, subtle spices with toasted sweet-corn, raspberries, and Demerera sugar finishing with creamy toffee, butterscotch, comb honey, and a floral flourish.

Other bourbons

A. Smith Bowman distillery

Fredericksburg, Virginia

Tel: 540 373 4555, www.asmithbowman.com

Built in 1935 in Fairfax County, the distillery was moved 60 miles to the north to its present location, in response to growth in 1988.

» **Bowman Brothers Virginia Bourbon**
Sweet-corn, surprisingly, and an almost rhubarb-crumble fruitiness and freshness with a creamy butter touch; the flavor is sweet, smooth, and of medium to good body with a little oaky vanilla; finishing with some heat and fresh fruit.

Tuthilltown Spirits distillery

Gardiner, New York

Tel: 845 633 8734, www.tuthilltown.com

Set up in 2003, Tuthilltown became New York's first distillery since Prohibition, prior to which, according to the company, there were "upwards of 1,000 farm stills." They produce small amounts using harvests from the farms in the area around the distillery.

» **Hudson's Four Grain Bourbon (2010 bottling)**
Juicy slices of orange sitting on top of creamy, buttered toast with a drizzle of maple syrup, it has a floral note and hint of fresh peach; the flavor is smooth and of spicy sweet-corn and fresh citrus finishing with mouth-watering, zesty orange and toasted marshmallows.

Tennessee style

The difference between bourbon and Tennessee whiskeys is that Tennessee whiskey is filtered through 10 feet of maple charcoal. The company claims that Jack Daniel's discovered the process, but it is also claimed that the practice was already common even before 1825, when it was recorded that Alfred Eaton had adopted the process.

Jack Daniel's distillery

Lynchburg, Moore County, Tennessee

Tel: 502 839 3436, www.jackdaniels.com

The world's largest whiskey distiller, Jack Daniel's annual production is now 180 million liters of alcohol, and sales are in excess of 10 million cases per annum. The population of Lynchburg is currently around a mere 500, of whom Jack Daniel's employs 370. Moore County is a "dry" county and the distillery visitor shop is the only outlet in Moore County that is permitted to sell liquor. It is also the top-selling liquor outlet in the state of Tennessee!

» **Jack Daniels Single Barrel**
For a distillery with an output as large as JD's, it is astounding that they can be bothered with such small-volume bottling runs as Single Barrel. Cherries, cream soda, coconut, some smoky cough-syrup character; the flavor is sweet and spicy, of good body, rich and chocolate orange; finishing with some spicy caramel oak and a floral note on the tail.

George Dickel distillery

Cascade Hollow, Tullahoma, Tennessee

Tel: 931 857 3124, www.dickel.com

In 1870, George Dickel set up as a distiller at Cascade Hollow on the Highland Rim of the Cumberland Plateau. A great experimenter, he found that the whisky (spelled this way as he felt that his whisky was comparable to Scotch whisky) he made in the winter was smoother than the summer's distillation, so he chilled his whisky before it went into the charcoal mellowing vats. The practice filters out the oils and fatty acids inherent in most whiskey products.

» ### George Dickel No. 12

EXPERT *Essential* Quite soft, sweet and buttery with walnut, peanut, toffee, and sweet-corn over charred oak; the flavor is of good weight, sweet, brown sugar with dried banana and coconut, vanilla oak and custard and darker treacle, finishing with a note of cinnamon, some raisins, caramel, honey, and the char replaying.

» ### George Dickel Barrel Select

Quite delicate, but charred oaky vanilla initially opening to leather, orange and licorice; the flavor is soft, smooth, and medium-bodied with sweet maple syrup, peppery spices, and beeswax; finishing quite elegantly ethereal with toffeed oak char and some citrus freshness.

Rye whiskey

Rye is a completely different category. Rye must be made from a mash bill containing a minimum of 51 percent rye and must be matured in new oak barrels. It makes a great base for cocktails because rye gives the whiskey a more spicy and characterful flavor than bourbon.

» **Jim Beam Rye**
Peppery rye and a little toffee apple and dried banana; the flavor is fresh, but light and smooth with a little orange finishing with medium length, some fennel and a little sweetness.

Rye revival

During Prohibition, American consumers sought alternatives to their non-available favorite liquors. They found that the spirits that were being smuggled across the Canadian border by the likes of the Kennedys and Al Capone were lighter and easier to drink than the whiskeys that they had been accustomed to prior to 1920. The result was that, after Prohibition's repeal, the heavily-flavored rye went out of fashion and the change in consumer taste to lighter-styled spirits caused rye almost to disappear.

Pikesville Rye

Produced by Heaven Hill in the Maryland style. Quite full, with caramel, sweet, leathery oak and acetone, and ripe pears at the back; the flavor is medium-sweet and of good weight with peppery spice, beeswax, and a dried apple note, and it finishes with the peppery rye and some citrus.

Rittenhouse Rye

Produced by Heaven Hill, in the style of the classic Pennsylvania or "Monongahela" rye whiskeys. Big and sweet, orange marmalade and ginger, cocoa/chocolate and toasted leather; the flavor is also quite big-bodied with dried citrus fruits, Demerara sugar, apples, and molasses; finishing dryish and spicy with a pleasant bitterness.

Sazerac Rye

EXPERT *Essential* Distilled by Buffalo Trace. Sweet vanilla spices leap out of the glass, followed by cloves, pepper, and cinnamon; the flavor is warm, medium-sweet, and rich with citrus and dipping toffee, finishing lingeringly and quite complex with licorice and a touch of paprika.

» **Van Winkle Family Reserve**
This is a 13-year-old whiskey produced at Buffalo Trace. Quite big with vanilla, sweet-corn, milk chocolate/cocoa, leather, and peppery spice; the flavor is medium-sweet with cherries, toffee apple and a hazelnut note. It finishes well with a hint of alcohol and caramel oak notes.

Other whiskey styles

Micro-distillation of whiskey has developed on the back of micro-brewing and fruit spirit distillation in the US, as elsewhere. The emphasis is on the "micro," with bottling runs being tiny and the consequent lack of availability of the whiskey.

Anchor Brewing Co.

San Francisco, California

Tel 415 863 8350, www.anchorbrewing.com

A microbrewery in the heart of San Francisco, Anchor branched out into micro-distilling in 1993 with the installation of small copper pot stills.

» **Old Potrero Rye**
Very smoky and similar to Scotch whisky. Old leather and Demerara sugar with some cinnamon; the flavor is rich and Christmas-cake fruity, buttery and spicy; finishing sweet with spiced fruits and a hint of smoke on the tail.

Clear Creek distillery

Portland, Oregon

Tel: 503 248 9470, www.clearcreekdistillery.com

Originally developed by Steve McCarthy, to produce fruit spirits from his family's orchards. He picked up a taste for peated whiskey after a wet visit to Ireland. His wash is produced by a local brewery.

» McCarthy's Oregon Single Malt

 Medium-bodied and youthful with a slightly green vegetal note, some apple, an earthily smoky peat note, a hint of rubber, and some candle wax; the flavor is medium-sweet and fresh with good peat integration, a touch of tarry rope and toffee and ripe citrus; finishing long, squeaky clean, rich and herby with bergamot and tea on the tail.

St. George's distillery

Alameda, California

Tel: 510 769 1601, www.stgeorgespirits.com

Set up in 1982 by Jörg Rupf from Alsace to distill eaux de vie. Having produced fruit spirits (a great deal of experimentation goes on in Alameda), it was natural that they should branch out into whiskey.

St. George Californian Single Malt

Very fruity—lime/cherries/red fruits—and a winey note with some buttery toffee and bubblegum; the flavor is medium-sweet with apples, blackberries, cloves, licorice and finishes with a little Szechuan spice and a reprise of the cherry bubblegum.

» International whiskeys

International expansion

While the British Isles (and Ireland) produced the world's original whiskeys, the rest of the world wasn't slow in catching up. The Japanese industry began in 1929 and other countries have been quick to follow. In more recent years, the growth in boutique micro-distilleries has been quite amazing to see.

Japan

The Japanese whiskey industry began in 1929; it developed out of the shochu and sake industries. Japanese distillers operate in a similar manner to the Irish in that they have a variety of different still shapes and styles in their stillhouses and by running the changes, can produce a wide variety of different flavors from the same stillhouse.

Chichibu distillery

Chichibu-shi, Saitama

Tel: +81(0)494 62 4601

Japan's newest distillery, producing first in 2008, the washbacks are made of the local Mizunara oak and the stills are from Forsyths in Rothes.

» **Chichibu Newborn Cask no. 446**

EXPERT *Essential* Quite big-bodied, sweet and rich with clean vanilla notes; with water, the bourbon notes really come out with hazelnut and maple predominating and a dark nutty note. The flavor is medium-dry, ripe, dark, and smooth with honey and spice bouncing across the tongue and some rich butterscotch; finishing long and slightly perfumed, very softly chewy and quite ethereal.

>> **Chichibu Heavily Peated**
Quite big-bodied with a breakfast cereal note and an aroma of smoked cheese, which becomes more smoked ham with the addition of water; the flavor is dry, quite rich, and gently chewy with a smoky cereal touch finishing long, powerful and heavily smoked.

Hakushu Higashi distillery

Hokuto, Yamanashi-ken

Tel: +81(0)551 35 2212

Built in 1981 to the west of the original Hakushu, which now only produces whiskey for blending. Suntory has established a bird reserve around the distillery, which is located in a forest at the southern end of the Japanese Alps.

>> **Hakushu 12 Years Old**
Medium-bodied and quite delicate with notes of peaches, orange blossom, honey, and citrus zest. The flavor is medium-dry and softly chewy showing chocolate, a floral note, and delicate peat; finishing very well with quite smoky, cocoa-flavored peat and espresso coffee on the tail.

Karuizawa distillery

Kitasakogun, Nagano

Tel: +81(0)267 320 0288

Built in a tourist region at the foot of an active volcano in 1955, the ivy-clad walls help to lower the buildings' internal temperatures during the area's hot summers. Karuizawa is currently closed and it seems that there is little prospect of it re-opening.

» **Karuizawa 17 Years Old**

Quite big-bodied, fruity, and rich with cough syrup and leafy orange notes backed by mahogany and brown sugar; the flavor is dry and gently chewy with soft peat, a little spice, and some citrus; finishing long with softly chewy oak tannins and dark, cocoa-flavored peat.

Yamazaki distillery

Shimamoto-cho, Mishama-gun, Osaka

Tel: +81(0)75 961 1234, www.theyamazaki.jp

Japan's first whiskey distillery, set up by Shinjiro Torii and Masataka Taketsuru in 1923 in an area that is surrounded by three rivers, giving ideal humidity. Owner Suntory uses a lot of Mizunara, the indigenous Japanese oak, casks for maturing their whiskeys.

» **Yamazaki 18 Years Old**

Quite delicate with mature sherry notes, rich dried fruit, orange peel, honey, and dark, but delicate peat; the flavor is medium-bodied, rich, and medium-dry with a wee bit of spice, some citrus, dried fruit, and a gentle brush of peat; finishing softly chewy, elegant, and quite ethereal.

» **Yamazaki 1984**

Lots of Mizunara flavor—sandalwood, incense, chocolate, licorice opens out and there is creamy toffee, some orange, and leathery vanilla; the flavor is medium-dry with Mizunara characters of pine, Japanese spices, and nuts backed up by plum jam and treacle. It finishes long, big-bodied, and complex, incense with notes of Japanese seaweed and candle wax.

Yoichi distillery

Yoichigun, Yoichimachi, Kurokawacho

Tel: +81(0)135 23 3131, www.nikka.com

Founded in 1934 by Masataka Taketsuru near the neck of the Shakotan Peninsula. He started with one pot still; he did not have enough money for a second still until some years later. Both distillations were carried out in this one still. Taketsuru felt that the humidity, water supply, and climate are similar to Scotland and the buildings have a very Scottish appearance.

» **Taketsuru 21 Years Old**

Medium-bodied, rich, sweet, oily oak, peaches and apricot jam, honey, and beeswax opens out along with buttery brioche/crème brûlée; the flavor is smooth, medium-sweet, and rounded with notes of orange marmalade, ginger, bergamot, and some spice; finishing long, with sweet spices and apricot jam, some fresh spearmint, and a hint of peat.

In the details

Using native wood casks
in the process of Japanese
whiskey making

» Mizunara magic

Over the centuries, oak has proved to be the best vessel for maturation to the extent that often, to count as a whiskey, it must be matured in an oak barrel.

In recent years, Japanese distilleries have looked to their indigenous strain of oak, which is known within Japan as "Mizunara" and have been aging some of their whiskeys in Mizunara casks. Unfortunately, this oak is in demand by Japanese furniture manufacturers and is not so plentiful as either American white oak or European oak, so its wood tends to be more expensive than its alternatives. It also requires more care in the handling, as Mizunara casks have a tendency to leak more readily.

Despite these drawbacks, Mizunara casks are in demand from Japanese distillers because of the overlay of sandalwood or incense flavors that the wood gives to the whiskey. The wood enhances Japanese whiskey's uniqueness.

Canada

Settlers from the Old World brought their distilling experiences with them, and Canada's vast acreage of grain production gave them cereals aplenty to mash. Canadian whiskeys are blended. Each grain gives a different character, as does each barrel.

Alberta distillery

Calgary, Alberta

Tel: 403 265 2541

Calgary is too cold to grow corn, so the whiskeys produced here have always had a high rye content. Rye whiskeys are not to everyone's taste; corn produces a soft, lighter, easier-drinking style of whiskey, but Alberta has doggedly stuck with its spicy style.

Alberta Premium

A little subdued with a floral touch, some honeyed toffee, chocolate, and glucose confectionery; the flavor is mellow, medium-sweet with some ginger and has a smooth and spicy rye bite and creamy vanilla, finishing cleanly and of medium length.

Canadian Mist distillery

Collngwood, Ontario

Tel: 705 445 4690, www.canadianmist.com

The stills here are outwardly made of shiny stainless steel, but their innards are constructed out of copper, so that the spirit is in contact with copper all through the distillation process. The spirit is triple-distilled and the mash bill is corn and barley to which a little rye whiskey made onsite is added.

>> **Canadian Mist**
Medium-bodied with a grassy fruitiness, lemons, oranges, vanilla, a malty note, and some cinnamon; the flavor is gentle, medium-sweet, and soft with creamy vanilla toffee and zingily fresh orange and a little spice; finishing clean and peppery with a little reprise from the lemon.

Crown Royal distillery

Gimli, Manitoba

Tel: 204 642 5123, www.crownroyal.com

Known as Gimli distillery until recently, the current distillery was opened only in 1968, the whiskey having been previously produced in the now-defunct Waterloo distillery in Ontario.

>> **Crown Royal Cask No. 16**
Medium-bodied, rich, and with some spice— nutmeg, ginger, and hazelnuts, green apples and a little peach; the flavor is sweet with juicy and zesty orange notes and softly chewy, creamy oak; finishing with buttery vanilla and a reprise of the sweet citrus.

Glenora distillery

Glenville, Inverness County, Nova Scotia

Tel: 902 258 2662, www.glenoradistillery.com

The distillery's make is a single malt produced in pot stills and is the only Scottish-style single malt made in Canada. The distillery, which opened in 1990 and is attached to a country inn, has the capacity to produce 250,000 liters of alcohol a year but normally produces just 50,000 liters annually.

>> **Glen Breton 10 Years Old Single Malt**
Big-bodied, creamy vanilla, and cereal notes, some butterscotch, honey, and pine notes; the flavor is rich, medium-sweet, and creamy with toffee and some chocolate spread on toast; finishing elegant, rounded and distinguished with a touch of sweetness and a breath of peat.

Highwood distillery

High River, Alberta

Tel: 403 652 3202, www.highwood-distillers.com

A Canadian independent distiller, described as "quirky." Established in 1974 it was originally called "Sunnyvale," but in 1984 was renamed "Highwood

Sampling a cask

In order to get a small amount out of a cask to sample, the industry developed a form of large pipette (known as a "valinch" from the Gaelic in Scotland and Ireland and as a "whiskey thief" in North America). These are made of copper with a small hole at the bottom and a vent hole at the top. The implement is inserted in the cask and fills with whiskey. The sampler covers the top hole with his thumb to create a vacuum, holding the whiskey within the tube, which can then be lifted out of the cask.

Distillers" after the famous river. Highwood uses Canadian prairie wheat instead of corn in the mash bills for its whiskeys.

›› Centennial 10 Years Old Rye

The nose is of apples and almonds sitting in toffee with a little garnish of orange peel; the flavor is fresh, smooth, and medium-dry with beeswax and some black pepper; finishing cleanly with the spice tingling across your tongue.

Kittling Ridge distillery

Grimsby, Ontario

Tel: 905 945 9225

Whiskey maker John Hall is an award-winning winemaker who has broadened his vision to produce a whiskey from his pot still distillery on Lake Ontario. He distills and matures each grain separately and then blends them to produce his ultimate whiskey.

›› Forty Creek Barrel Select

EXPERT *Essential* Rich and delicately sherried with a charred cask note and fruity—orange, cherry, and chocolate with brown sugar; the flavor is rich and honeyed with butterscotch and coffee, finishing subtly and cleanly with a little cocoa on the tail.

Valleyfield distillery

Salaberry-de-Valleyfield, Quebec

Tel: 450 373 3230

The V.O. stands for "Very Own" and the brand was originally created for the Seagram family's exclusive use. The Seagram company is no longer in existence; the distillery is now owned by Pernod Ricard.

» **Seagram V.O.**

Spicy, young, fruity, apples and apricot, well-integrated corn, and cinnamon; the flavor is medium-dry and smooth with marmalade oranges, zingy acidity, and honey; finishing clean and warm with a bitter touch on the end.

Walkerville distillery

Walkerville, Ontario

Tel: +1(0)519 561 5499

Hiram Walker, driven out of Detroit by the temperance movement, started construction near Windsor, Ontario in 1857. A town called Walkerville grew up around the distillery. During Prohibition in the US, Canadian whiskey became very popular and the proximity of Detroit made it easy for the company to profit from it.

» **Canadian Club**

Sweet-corn/vanilla custard with some orange and spice; the flavor is medium-bodied, sweet, and rye spicy supported by the malted barley, and it finishes clean with some bitter rye.

Europe

Penderyn distillery

Penderyn, Wales

Tel: +44(0)1685 810651, www.welsh-whiskey.co.uk

Penderyn is the first distillery operational in Wales since the late 19th century and is located in the heart of the Brecon Beacons National Park. It uses a unique form of still that is very energy efficient; it has a traditional pot beneath a tall rectifying column. Their wash is supplied by Welsh brewer S A Brain & Co.

» **Penderyn Welsh Whiskey Sherrywood**
Fresh, clean, and unpeated with slight floral and rich, quite dark fruit notes, a little pepper, toffee, beeswax, and green apple skins. The flavor is medium-dry with an edge of sweetness and clean with a touch of spice tingling across the tongue; finishing creamy with caramel, ginger, and honey notes.

St. George's distillery

Roudham, Norfolk

Tel: +44(0)1953 717939,
www.englishwhiskey.co.uk

A farming family with 600 years history of growing and processing grain, the Nelstrops opened their distillery late in 2006 on land down by the River Thet. They pulled in Iain Henderson, who had just retired after 30 years distilling in Scotland, to oversee the spirit production.

St. George's Chapter 9

Medium-bodied with a smoky, charred oak note; water brings out the sweetness and delicate lime and apricot fruit; the flavor is medium-dry, with the sweetness growing, of good weight with rich vanilla and finishing cleanly and quite complex with smoky spices and chocolate.

Glann ar Mor distillery

Crec'h ar Fur, Brittany

Tel: +33(0)296 16 58 08, www.glannarmor.com

Installed, in 2005, into a farmhouse that was built in 1668 in the Presqu'ile Sauvage (the Wild Peninsula) of northern Brittany. On a sea-battered coastline, a former advertising executive from Paris has established this distillery.

Glann ar Mor Second Bottling

Medium-bodied and fruity with a youthful bubblegum note, cocoa comes out followed by desiccated coconut and acetone; the flavor is medium-sweet, of good weight, and rich with a delicate peat note, some honey, bubblegum, and slightly biscuity—chocolate digestives; finishing long, very clean, and quite ethereal with a slight hint of menthol.

Zuidam distillery

Baarle Nassau, the Netherlands

Tel: +31 13 507 8470, www.zuidam.eu

Established in 1975, the barley is ground using traditional Dutch windmills. The family began as distillers of genever and produced their first whiskey in 2000. They have four small pot stills, which are also used for the production of their other spirits.

>> **Millstone 8 Years Old French Oak**

EXPERT *Essential* Medium-bodied and rich with good apple/peach and citrus fruit notes. There is a perfumed character, some floral notes, and coconut sitting at the back; the flavor is dry, with good body, cocoa, cereal, and dry paper; finishing long and dry with nutty toffee and coconut.

Mackmyra distillery

Valbo, Sweden

Tel: +46(0)26 54 18 80, www.mackmyra.com

Now 10 years old, Mackmyra was set up in a former power station. Juniper twigs are added to the peat when drying the malt, and Swedish barley and Swedish oak casks are used. Maturation occurs in cool conditions 150 feet underground in a former mine.

>> **Mackmyra Preludium 06**

Quite forward fruit characters of lemon and pear backed by some juniper, toffee, honey, and woodsmoke; the flavor is fresh, smoky, and malty with a strong vanilla oak note and finishing with toasted oak and firm cinnamon spice.

Rest of the world

Bakery Hill distillery

Balwyn North, Victoria, Australia,

+61 3 98577070, www.bakeryhilldistillery.com.au

Established in a north-eastern suburb of Melbourne in 1999, Bakery Hill's preferred strain of barley is the local Schooner and their whiskeys mature quickly because of the small size of their 50- or 100-liter casks.

» **Bakery Hill Cask Strength Peated Malt**
Quite soft, delicate, and medium-bodied with notes of baked red-skinned apples with cloves and a delicate, perfumed peat character; the flavor is medium-dry with gently chewy apple skins, very Calvados-like with some citrus and it finishes with a little touch of spice, smoke, and a hint of cocoa.

Tasmania distillery

Cambridge, Tasmania,

+61 3 62485399, www.tasmaniadistillery.com

Originally situated at Sullivan's Cove, the business was purchased by a group of enthusiasts in 2003 and moved to Cambridge, on the outskirts of Hobart. Their wash is produced for them from the Franklin strain of barley at Hobart's Cascade Brewery.

» **Sullivan's Cove Double Cask**
Quite full and youthful with a chocolate malty note and a rancio character; there are chocolate raisins, a touch of citrus, and rich, honeyed vanilla; the flavor is medium-dry, rich, and smooth with a smoky

Words from the wise

Ralf Mitchell Commentator,
www.ralfy.com

» A time and a place

There is a whiskey for different times of day, weather, and occasion, and a connoisseur needs to get it right. The weight of a whiskey in your mouth determines where that whiskey will sit in the drinking sensory firmament.

If you are entertaining whiskey enthusiasts, a light, delicate whiskey such as Cutty Sark, Auchentoshan, or the Californian St. George's might not be very well received, but these same whiskeys would be applauded by a mixed gathering for a light lunch in the sun. The enthusiasts would love the Caol Ila 18 Years Old, Glenfarclas 21 Years Old, or Glann ar Mor Kornog, and were you to serve Wild Turkey 101 or Springbank 15 Years Old at a high-profile dinner, then your prestige would be very solidly established. Like everything in life, you have to tailor your choice to your audience.

chocolate character; finishing with quite good length with a little touch of spice, some cream soda, and ripe peaches.

James Sedgwick distillery

Wellington, South Africa

Tel: +27(0)21 873 1161

This is the first blend of South African malt and grain whiskeys. After initial maturation, the blend is filled into first-fill bourbon casks for a further maturation.

» **Three Ships Bourbon Cask Finish**
Vanilla oak, some perfume and spice, a very bourbon-influenced nose; the flavor is bourbon-like, with pepper, creamy vanilla, and a floral touch to the finish, which is quite light and medium-dry with a touch of maple syrup.

Amrut distillery

Rajajinigar, Bangalore

Tel: +91(0)80 2310 0379,
www.amrutdistilleries.com

Amrut first distilled whiskey for blending in the early 1980s using barley grown in the Punjab and Rajasthan. Their first single malt was released in 2004.

» **Amrut Fusion**
This is quite rich and toffeed with an orange perfume and a peat note that floats above the rest; the flavor has fresh, leathery, beeswax-coated oak, is medium-dry, smooth, and gently chewy, supported by creamy beeswax. It has a clean and very impressive finish with a tang of the peat smoke.

» Independent bottlers

The Independents

The independent bottlers grew out of the whiskey-broking side of the whiskey industry and have predominantly originated in Scotland.

An independent bottler is a business that buys casks of whiskey, either as newly filled casks that must be laid down to mature, or else as a part of an unrequired parcel of casks. The independent bottler will then have the contents of these casks filled into bottles when it considers the whiskey to be ready.

Many of these companies are relatively small, family-owned businesses; many of their bottlings are of single casks, yielding a small number of bottles and, therefore, are very close to unrepeatable as each cask imposes a slightly different thumbprint on the whiskey inside it. Most of the independents interfere with the whiskey as little as possible, so very few nowadays add E150, the caramel coloring used in many commercial bottlings, and few chill-filter.

A commercial bottler may bottle between 100 and 200 casks of its 12-year-old whiskey; this averages out the flavor characteristics of the individual cask, allowing the distiller to make a flavor statement and impose a signature, which can be very closely replicated in the next bottling. The independent bottler, because of the small number of bottles involved, is interacting with the more informed consumer who appreciates the uniqueness of the single cask and the independent's bottling.

Directory of bottlers

Berry Brothers & Rudd

3 St. James Street, London, W6 9RW, UK

Tel: +44 (0)800 2802440, www.bbr.com

The company, originally established in 1698, now owns The Glenrothes brand and holds a Royal Warrant to supply alcoholic beverages to the Queen. It has bottled whiskeys under its own "Berry's Own Selection" label for in excess of 100 years.

Wm Cadenhead

83 Longrow, Campbeltown, Argyll, PA28 6EX, UK

Tel: +44 (0)1585 54258, www.wmcadenhead.com

Scotland's oldest firm of independent bottlers and therefore at the forefront of single malt marketing. It has stores in Edinburgh, London, and Campbeltown and franchises across Europe.

Cárn Mòr

Scottish Liqueur Centre, Hilton, Bankfoot, Perthshire, PH1 4EB, UK

Tel: +44 (0)1738 787044, www.scottish-liqueur-centre.com

The new boy on the block, and a tourist destination, the center bottled its first casks in 2007, but the management's previous whiskey expertise means that this now forms an important part of the business.

Compass Box Delicious Whisky Ltd.

9 Power Road, London, W4 5YN, UK

Tel: +44 (0)2089 950899,
www.compassboxwhiskey.com

This company, established by Minnesotan John Glaser, produces innovative and imaginative bottlings. He has been referred to as the Scotch whisky industry's *bête noire* because of his attempts to drag the industry into the 21st century. He doesn't believe in age statements but bottles when he considers the whiskeys to be ready. His labels are Peat Monster, Spice Tree, Oak Cross, and Hedonism.

A. Dewar Rattray Ltd.

Whitefaulds Farm, Culzean Road, Ayrshire,
KA19 8AH, UK

Tel: +44 (0)1655 885756, www.dewarrattray.com

Founded in 1868 as an importer of French wines, Italian spirits and olive oil, the business was returned to the family of one of its founders in 2004 when it was bought by Tim Morrison. They now specialize single malt whiskeys and their own label, Stronachie.

Ian Macleod Distillers Ltd.

Russell House, Dunnet Way, Broxburn,
EH52 5BU, UK

Tel: +44 (0)1506 852205, www.ianmacleod.com

Originally a subsidiary company of Edinburgh brokers Peter J. Russell, Ian Macleod is now the major part of the business, owning Glengoyne distillery and the Isle of Skye blend.

Words from the wise

Keir Sword Owner, Royal Mile
Whiskies, Scotland

» Obtaining limited bottlings

We don't need to stock everything. If one distillery
has 15 different bottlings, we will stock what we
think we will need. Our customers know that we will
make every effort to source and obtain the bottles
they are looking for but, fortunately, they realize that
we don't have an unlimited storage space.

Having said that, limited bottlings are regularly
greatly over-subscribed and often sold out on the day
that they are released. To be fair to everybody, we
will not accept advance orders for something that is
going to be in very short supply. We will know in
advance of the release date when that release date
will be, so we will advise anyone who expresses an
interest that they must contact us after a certain time
on the release date. Then our customers will have a
fair chance of getting their hands on these elusive
and exclusive bottlings.

The Scotch Single Malt Circle

c/o W. Miller, Auf der Hofreith 35, D- 40489
Düsseldorf, Germany

Tel: +49(0)21 140 0153, www.scotchsingle.de

Set up by Bill Miller and his wife, Maggie, in 1983, as a small club celebrating the produce of his homeland, the Circle now bottles a wide range of casks annually.

Scotch Malt Sales

1-8-4, Itabashi , Itabashi-ku,
Tokyo 173-0004, Japan

Tel.: +81(0)3 3579 8587, www.scotch-malt.co.jp

Established in 1971 as Oasaka Ltd., the company became the Japanese importer for Morrison Bowmore in 1979 and, in 1982, it changed its name. It began to import small casks of Scotch whisky in 1983.

The Scotch Malt Whisky Society

The Vaults, 7 Giles Street, Edinburgh, EH6 6BZ,
UK

Tel: +44 (0)131 554 3451, www.smws.co.uk

This Edinburgh-based society bottles cask-strength whiskys for its members. Each cask is bottled under a numerical code, so as not to identify the source distillery on the label. The Society now has branches in Australia, Austria, France, Germany, Italy, Japan, the Netherlands, South Africa, Sweden, Switzerland, Taiwan, and the US.

Speyside Distillers Co. Ltd.

Duchess Road, Rutherglen, Glasgow, G73 1AU, UK

Tel: +44 (0)1416 474464,
www.speysidedistillery.co.uk

A brand name used by owners of Speyside distillery for a selection of single malt whiskeys, originally selected by Robert Scott, their former distiller.

The Signatory Vintage Malt Whisky Company

Edradour Distillery, Pitlochry, Perthshire, PH16 5JP, UK

Tel: +44 (0)17 9647 2095, www.edradour.co.uk

Established by Andrew Symington in Leith in 1988, Signatory bought Edradour distillery in 2002 and now is located there, where they have built a bottling hall.

Cask characteristics

Whiskey barrels are made by hand from oak, and the thickness of the staves will vary from cask to cask. Therefore no cooper or distiller will guarantee the exact quantity contained within a cask.

The staves are curved by the application of flame, which softens the cellulose from which the wood is constructed and allows it to be bent. Sherry casks are toasted on the inside, which allows more of the wood tannins to flavor the whiskey, while bourbon casks are charred, caramelizing the cellulose to give the spirit a sweet, vanilla note.

Van Wees Whisky World

Leusderweg 260, Amersfoot, 3817 KH, The Netherlands

Tel: + (0)33 461 6426, www.whiskyworld.nl

In 1963, this wine-importing house began importing Scotch whisky and in 1995 began bottling its own selections under "The Ultimate Single Malt Scotch Whisky Selection" label.

The Vintage Malt Whisky Company

2 Stewart Street, Milngavie, Glasgow, G62 6BW, UK

www.vintagemaltwhiskey.com

Set up by Brian Crook in 1992, the company bottles its single malt selections under the "Cooper's Choice" label and also owns the brands Finlaggan, Tantallan, and Glen Almond.

Wilson & Morgan Ltd.

24 Great King Street, Edinburgh, EH3 6QN, UK

www.wilsonandmorgan.com

Established by the Rossi family from Italy in 1992. The family had imported Scotch whisky into Italy for many years before setting up their own series of labels for mature bottling.

Enjoying whiskey

Distillery employees spend many years of their lives in a distillery. Over these years, their understanding and mastery of the process is enhanced and improved. All of this expertise goes into making the finest whiskey possible for your drinking pleasure.

However, some people focus on collecting whiskey for its own sake, building up formidable collections of bottles of whiskeys. Mainly because of this mania for collecting, the price of rare—and not so rare—bottlings have increased and, in some cases, increased quite considerably.

The product of certain distilleries, The Macallan and Bowmore to name but two, has leaped up in price in the past 20 years. Ardbeg has always been desirable for Islay fans; historically, this is because bottlings of the distillery's make were rare and, when a new bottling was made available, it disappeared almost immediately.

But whiskey is meant to be drunk and enjoyed. It is a gregarious spirit meant for sharing in good company. It is not meant to sit in a bottle and be looked at. If that were the case, the spirit-making expertise of all those distillery employees would be unnecessary.

Bottlings and age

A company's core bottling is the one upon which its reputation depends. You will find therefore that this is its most consistent product, as it cannot afford to alienate those consumers who have come to rely on this brand as their "usual." Other bottlings will very often use a smaller, often considerably smaller, number of casks in their vatting. As such, there will be variations in color and flavor between bottlings, but, as the market for these bottlings is (naturally) smaller and more informed, these variations are accepted and often even expected.

The more mature bottlings at, say, 21, 25, 30 years old, or older, will differ from their predecessors. As a result of sales of that distillery's whiskeys over the years and the amount that the angels consume, there is frequently a lack of availability of sufficient stocks of a particular color or flavor profile and, in a 25-year-old bottling, it may be necessary to include a cask of a 40-year-old whiskey, just to maintain some consistency in the bottling.

Life is easier for a blender putting together a vatting of, for example, Chivas Royal 25 Years Old. The blender will be able to change his recipe if whiskey from distillery X is not available; by adding some from distillery Y and some from distillery Z, he can obtain the character he is looking for.

Styles of whiskey

Naturally, you will find a style of whiskey that you are comfortable with, that you will sip happily until your dying day.

The easiest whiskeys to drink are the sweetest, and because of this, they satisfy the most palates. Some of the cognoscenti will argue that these are the simplest whiskeys, but that is not the case. Into the sweetest category fit most bourbons, most Speyside malts, a number of blends of Scotch and Irish and some Japanese.

The cask has a great influence on the sweetness of the final spirit; the previous inhabitant of a cask will influence sweetness levels in your whiskey. First-fill bourbon or first-fill oloroso sherry will heighten sweetness levels, second- or third-fill less so.

At the other end of the scale are most Islay whiskeys or heavily peated others. This is a category you will either love or hate; there are really no fence-sitters with peat smoke. Current understanding of cask influence has added more complex characters and made the peat hit more subtle than was the case 30 years ago, but peat flavor is still something that completely divides opinion amongst whiskey drinkers.

American or Canadian rye whiskeys, with their spicy, grainy flavors, are not as easy to get into as the soft, almost decadent bourbons, but many of them are well worth that little bit of effort on your part.

Buying at auction

Since the first dedicated whiskey auction was held at Christie's in Bath Street, Glasgow in 1989, prices have escalated. Collectors from around the world have flocked to the auction houses to snap up the bargains to be had there. Nowadays, bidders for these magnificent bottlings no longer have to make the trek to Glasgow or Edinburgh to attend the auctions in person; they can stay at home and bid online. One benefit is that this means that the auction rooms should be less crowded, but it also means that there are more people bidding and likely to push up the prices of the bottles in which you are interested. This all means that, at the moment, the market in "collectable" whiskeys is very healthy, but as with any tradeable item, the value can go down as well as up.

Major international auction houses

Bonham's
www.bonhams.com

Christie's
www.christies.com

McTear's
www.mctears.co.uk

Southeby's
www.sothebys.com

Buying at retail

Many retailers around the world offer a wide selection of whiskeys from all corners of the world and, likewise, most will despatch to all corners of the world. The major retailers have good websites.

NORTH AMERICA

Binny's Beverage Depot
300 North Clarke St, Lakeview, IL 60657, USA
773 935 9400, www.binnys.com

D&M Wines & Liquors
2200 Fillmore St, San Francisco, CA 94115, USA
415 346 1325, www.dandm.com

Dundee Dell
5007 Underwood Ave, Omaha, NE 68132, USA
402 553 9501, www.dundeedell.com

Park Avenue Liquors
292 Madison Ave, New York City, NY 10017, USA
212 685 2442, www.parkaveliquors.com

The Whisky Shop
360 Sutter St, San Francisco, CA 94108, USA
415 989 1030, www.whiskyshopusa.com

UNITED KINGDOM

Berry Bros. & Rudd
3 St James's Street, London, SW1A 1EG, England
+44 (0)800 2802440, www.bbr.com

The Cadenhead Whiskey Shop
172 Canongate, Edinburgh, EH8 8BN, Scotland
+44 (0)1315 565864,
http://edinburgh.wmcadenhead.com

Cadenhead's Covent Garden Whisky Shop
3 Russell St, London, WC2B 5JD, England
+44 (0)2079 356999,
www.coventgardenwhiskyshop.co.uk

Canape Wines
85 Main St, Bothwell, Glasgow, G71 8ER, Scotland
+44 (0)1698 854455, www.canapewines.co.uk

Duncan Taylor & Co. Ltd.
4 Upperkirkgate, Huntly, Aberdeenshire, AB54 8JU,
Scotland, +44 (0)1466 794055, www.duncantaylor.co.uk

Eaglesome Ltd., Reform Square
30–32 Reform Square, Campbeltown, Argyll, PA28 6JA,
Scotland, +44 (0)1586 551710

Gordon & MacPhail Ltd
58 South St, Elgin, Moray, IV30 1Y, Scotland
+44 (0)1343 545110, www.gordonandmacphail.com

Luvian's Bottle Shop
93 Bonnygate, Cupar, Fife, KY15 4LG, Scotland
+44 (0)1334 654820, www.luvians.com

Milroys
3 Greek St, Soho, London, W1A 1ER, England
+44 (0)207 4372385, www.milroys.co.uk

Royal Mile Whiskys
379/381 High St, Edinburgh, EH1 1PW, Scotland
+44 (0)1312 253383, www.royalmilewhiskys.com

Villeneuve Wines Ltd.
1 Venlaw Court, Peebles, EH45 8AE, Scotland
+44 (0)1721 722500, www.villeneuvewines.com

The Whisky Exchange
Vinopolis 1, Bank End, London, SE1 9BU England
+44 (0)2088 389388, www.thewhiskyexchange.com

EUROPE

Drankenshop Broekmans
Molenstraat 19, Zolder, Belgium
+32(0)11 53 70 60, www.drankenshop.be

Gall & Gall van der Boog
Dr H. Colijnlaan 289, Rijswijk, The Netherlands
www.gall.nl

Juul's Vinhandel
Værnedamsvej 15, 1819 Frederiksberg, Copenhagen,
Denmark +45 (0)33 31 13 29, www.juuls.dk

Kratochvílovci
T˝nská 15, Praha 1, Czech Republic
+42 (0)608 111 093, www.kratochvilovci.cz

La Maison du Whisky
20 rue d'Anjou, Paris, France
+33 (0)14265 0316, www.whisky.fr

Weinquelle Lühmann
Lübecker Str. 145, 22067 Hamburg, Germany
+49 (0)40 602 5234, www.weinquelle.com

Whisk(e)y Shop tara
Rindermarkt 16, 80331 München, Germany
+49 (0)89 265 118, www.whiskyversand.de

Vintage and rare whiskeys

As we have already said, any single cask bottling is, by its very nature, rare. The thickness of the staves, the number of cells in the wood, the location of the cask in the warehouse, the environment during maturation, the amount of handling the cask has received, climatic changes across the maturation period, even the length of time the whiskey spends in a vat before being put into the bottle—all of these combine to create a totally unique flavor profile. The subtle nuances contained in the flavor of the whiskey from that cask are not replicated in any of the casks filled on the same day and stored around it.

Having said that, these nuances are subtle. Most drinkers would not notice many of the differences. To be honest, most drinkers wouldn't even be interested in looking for these subtleties. The very fact that you are reading this book means that you are likely to be looking for these subtleties.

Single cask market

Many single cask bottling are quite reasonably priced, especially from independent bottlers. Diageo's Managers' Choice bottling, on the other hand, is a total of 27 bottlings, one from each of Diageo's distilleries (apart from Roseisle, which only came on stream in 2009) and their price point is taking full advantage of the collectors' market. An 8-year-old Oban for $450 a bottle, for example, is excessive.

The companies argue that these are the finest examples of whiskey from their respective distilleries, that collectors at auction would push the price up in any case, and there are a very limited number of bottles available for the whole world. In the case of the Oban, there are 534 bottles, while the cask of Teaninch yielded a mere 246 bottles. From the company's declaration, it seems unlikely that many of these bottles will be drunk and that, in the fullness of time, most will pass beneath an auctioneer's gavel.

Vintage casks

As to vintage, the difference between the character of, say, Scotland's excessively wet summer of 2010 and its excessively dry summer of 2003 has very little difference on the flavor except that the barley harvest in both vintages is put under stress; 2003 is reduced in size because of a lack of water and 2010 is reduced because of too much water in July and early August. Harvesting of summer barley in 2010, however, was under good conditions, so the quality was good.

The Glenrothes makers have focused on the vintage, and only show that on most of their labels and bottle their whiskey when they think these casks are at their peak. It is difficult to make an argument for vintage variations because due to the difference in age, the cask influence varies from bottling to bottling. You will find nuances of difference between, for example, the 1994 and the 1991, but a great many of these differences are down to the influence of the wood.

Similarly, Balblair is only available by the vintage and, for the three vintages of Balblair currently available, 1975, 1989, and 2000, Andy MacDonald, the distillery manager, nosed 1,062 casks to select a mere 81 casks for bottling.

Storing whiskey

There is not the same storage difficulty with whiskey that there is with wine. Oxidization is not so much of a problem, but, as with all alcohols, oxygen is a killer —alcohol and oxygen react to form acetic acid and water. Which means that, as soon as the bottle is opened, deterioration begins, as acetic acid is vinegar. With a bottle of wine, this may take 48 hours; the higher alcohol content of whiskey means that you may have as long as two years before it deteriorates to any great extent.

This also means that many bars, where a large number of spirits are offered, are offering a product that is past its best. Superior outlets, such as The Highlander Inn in Craigellachie on Speyside, impose a sell-by date on their bottles and they cut the price of whiskeys as they near that sell-by date in order to turn the stock over. In the case of The Highlander, they put a label on each bottle showing the date it was opened and, if it is not totally consumed within one year, it is consigned to kitchen duty.

Storage time

If unopened, a bottle can be stored almost indefinitely. Obviously, it should not be stored for a long period in direct sunlight. The liquid does not like that and the label will fade, reducing the value. If you are storing a bottle to benefit from its appreciation in value, it is essential that the carton, if any, is also stored and kept in good condition. The easiest way to do this is to store it in a cool, darkened area and wrap each item in cling film. This protects labels, cartons, and seals from unwelcome intrusion by beast, insects, and humans.

Avoiding damage in storage

I was asked to value a pub owner's considerable whiskey collection some years ago. On examining the bottles closely, I saw most of the seals had been broken. It seemed that some person had discovered this trove of bottles and, probably over several years, had sampled many of these and topped up the bottles with some other liquid. The publican was completely unaware of this and, initially, would not believe me until I clearly showed him that the capsules and seals moved where they shouldn't have. When I left him, the steam was still coming out of his ears and I felt that he was intent on committing violence towards whomsoever he thought had been the perpetrators of this crime.

Likewise, another retailer asked me to value his collection, which was stored in a damp cellar beneath his shop. Unfortunately, the damp had damaged several of the labels of some very expensive whiskeys, reducing their auction value considerably.

I reiterate my earlier claim that you should drink these bottles. That is what they were created for—enjoyment!

Whiskey cocktails

Whiskeys have long been a base for the most classic of cocktails, from sours, juleps, and Manhattans through to more exotic concoctions. These recipes all make one cocktail serving.

Manhattan

2 fl oz rye whiskey

1 fl oz dry vermouth

A dash of Angostura Bitters

Shake with ice and strain into a cocktail glass. Garnish with a slice of lemon peel.

Mint Julep

1 fl oz of a peated Scotch whisky

A dash of rhubarb bitters

A cube of sugar

Mint

St. Germain elderflower liqueur

Shake with crushed ice and serve in a tall glass with a garnish of mint. Serve with a straw.

Rob Roy

1 fl oz Scotch whisky

1 fl oz sweet vermouth

A dash of Angostura Bitters

Stir in a glass with ice and strain into a cocktail glass.

John Collins

2 fl oz Bourbon	
1 fl oz lemon juice	
1 teaspoon sugar syrup	
3 fl oz soda water	

Half fill a shaker with ice cubes. Add bourbon, lemon juice, and sugar syrup and shake. Strain into a tall glass almost filled with ice cubes. Add soda and stir. Garnish with a maraschino cherry and orange slice.

Shamrock

1 fl oz Irish whiskey	
1 fl oz dry vermouth	
3 dashes green Chartreuse	
3 dashes green crème de menthe	

Stir in a glass with ice and strain into a cocktail glass.

Whiskey Sour

1½ fl oz whiskey	
1½ fl oz lemon juice	
¾ fl oz sugar syrup	

Shake ingredients in a shaker with ice cubes. Strain into a tall glass. Garnish with a maraschino cherry.

»Discover

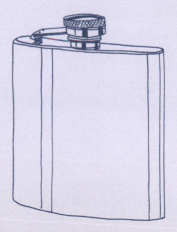

International appreciation

The only way to fully appreciate a whiskey is to visit the place of its creation. Most distilleries experience a dimunition of water supply in the warmer summer months and so tend to shut down production for a few weeks. So make sure before planning your trip you check when the distillery is closed.

Most of the world's distilleries are a little off the beaten track. Very few are, like Auchentoshan in Glasgow or Clear Creek in Portland, actually in cities. A number of very knowledgeable people, now run businesses that take you on visits to whiskey country.

Distillery Destinations Ltd.

304 Albert Drive, Glasgow, G41 5RS, Scotland

Tel: +44(0)1414 290762, www.whisky-tours.co.uk

Distillery Destinations is run by Caroline Dewar, who was head of P.R. at Allied Distillers for several years. She has written for numerous publications about whiskey, and also conducts lectures and tastings.

Christine Logan

39 Stanalane, Bowmore, Isle of Islay, PA43 7LA, Scotland

Tel: +44(0)1496 810485, www.ladyoftheisles.co.uk

Christine was in charge of Bowmore distillery's visitor center for some years. Her knowledge of Islay's distilleries, its wildlife, and history is profound.

Kentucky Bourbon Distillery Tours

www.bourbontrailtours.com

A company that organizes tours to the distilleries across the state, providing you with The Kentucky Bourbon Trail® Experience.

Tasting Events

There are many annual tasting events around the world organized by various companies, such as Whisky Live! in Tokyo in February, Whiskies of the World®Expo in San Francisco in March, WhiskyFest in Chicago in April, and the Limburg Whisky Fair in Germany in May. Visit the websites to see when the next events closest to you take place.

Whisky Live International Tasting Events
www.whiskylive.com

WhiskyFest USA
www.maltadvocate.com
www.whiskyfestblog.com

Scotch Malt Whisky Society
www.smws.co.uk

Speyside Whisky Festival
www.spiritofspeyside.com

Whiskies of the World
www.whiskiesoftheworld.com

The Whisky Fair
www.festival.whiskyfair.com/

World's best whiskey bars

While it is pleasant to just sit and sip on a whiskey in your own home, whiskey is a gregarious spirit and craves company. Where better to experience that than in the ambience of the world's finest whiskey bars?

NORTH AMERICA

Curragh Irish Pub, 73 East 8th St, Holland, MI 49423, USA

Char No. 4, 196 Smith St., Brooklyn, NY 11201, USA

Baxter Station, 1202 Payne St, Louisville, KY 40204, USA

Bourbons Bistro, 2255 Frankfort Ave, Louisville, KY 40206, USA

The Dam Pub, 53 Bruce St, Thornbury, Ontario NOH 2PO, Canada

Duke of Perth, 2913 N Clark St, Chicago, IL 60657, USA

Seven Grand, 515 West 7th St, Los Angeles, CA 90014, USA

St. Andrews Restaurant and Bar, 140, West 46th St, New York, NY 10036, USA

UNITED KINGDOM

Albannach 66 Trafalgar Square, London WC2N 5DS, England

The Anderson Union Street, Fortrose, Ross-shire, IV10 8TD, Scotland

The Bon Accord 153 North St, Glasgow, G3 7DA, Scotland

Bushmills Inn 9 Dunluce Road, Bushmills, BT57 8QG, Northern Ireland

Cherrybank Inn 210 Glasgow Road, Perth, PH2 0NA, Scotland

Drumchork Lodge Hotel Aultbea, Wester Ross, IV22 2HU, Scotland

The Fisherman's Retreat Riding Head Lane, Shuttleworth, Ramsbottom, Lancashire, BL0 0HH, England

The Grill 213 Union St, Aberdeen, AB11 6BA, Scotland

The Highlander Inn Craigellachie, Banffshire, AB38 9SR, Scotland

The Lismore 206, Dumbarton Road, Glasgow, G11 6UN, Scotland

The Lochside Hotel Shore Street, Bowmore, Isle of Islay, PA43 7LB, Scotland

Spirit Safe Visitors to the Glen Grant distillery will generally get a small measure of whisky to sample served in a plastic cup, and that will be that. Select guests to the distillery, however, will get to sample something a little more unique. The Glen Grant burn flows down the hill past Glen Grant distillery. In the latter part of the 19th century, James Grant the younger built a dram safe into the rocks at the side of this burn. Guests at dinner were encouraged to take a post-prandial stroll through the grounds of the major's home, and their path would take them through the gardens to where the burn flows through a small gorge. Here the major would stop and remove from the well-disguised safe a bottle of Glen Grant and some glasses. His enthralled audience would enjoy their dram diluted by the vigorous waters of the Glen Grant burn. The dram safe is still in use today, although you will have to be a very lucky visitor to taste a sample from it.

The Mash Tun 8, Broomfield Square, Aberlour, Banffshire, AB38 9QP, Scotland

The Munro Inn Strathyre, by Callander, Perthshire, FK18 8NA, Scotland

The Pot Still 154 Hope Street, Glasgow, G2 2TH, Scotland

The St. Andrews Bar 37 Sunnyside St, Coatbridge, Lanarkshire, ML5 3DG, Scotland

The Taychreggan Hotel 4 Ellieslea Road, Broughty Ferry, Dundee, DD5 1JG, Scotland

Whiski 119 High St, The Royal Mile, Edinburgh, EH1 1SG, Scotland

The Whisky Bar at the Caledonian Hotel Princes Street, Edinburgh, EH1 2AB, Scotland

EUROPE

138

BarMetro Via dei Martinitt, 3, Milan, Italy

The Beaufort Bar Beaufort, Killarney, Co. Kerry, Ireland

Brugs Whiskyhuis Cordoeaniersstraat 4, 8000 Brugge, Belgium

Hotel Fidder Kon. Wilhelminastraat 6, 8019 AM Zwolle, The Netherlands

North End Pub Noordeinde 55, 2311 CB Leiden, The Netherlands

O'Loclainn's Irish Whiskey Bar Ballyvaughan, Co. Clare, Ireland

The Temple Bar 47/48, Temple Bar, Dublin, Ireland

Wallace Bar 2, Rue Octavio Mey, Lyon 69005, France

Whiskycafe L&B Korte Leidsedwarsstr 82–84, 1017 RD Amsterdam, The Netherlands

ASIA

Bar Talisker Fujihira Building, B1F 7-5-12 Ginza, Chuo-Ku, Tokyo

The Harbour Inn Shibata 1-3-7 Shibata, Kita-ku, Osaka, Tokyo

The Highlander Inn Musashi-ya, 2-1-6 Chuo, Nakano-ku, Tokyo

The Mash Tun Kami-Osaki 2F, Shinagawa-ku, Tokyo

Whiskey education

To gain more whiskey knowledge, there are courses you can enroll in that will enable you to talk authoritatively and, more to the point, accurately on this complex subject. Courses lasting several days are held at a number of distilleries in Scotland where you can gain hands-on experience of making whisky, from malting through to filling the barrel with the spirit you have made.

The Whisky School at Bladnoch distillery
Bladnoch, Wigtown, Scotland, DG8 9AB
Tel: +44(0)1988 402235
www.bladnoch.co.uk/whisky-school

The Whisky Experience at Loch Ewe distillery
Drumchork Lodge Hotel, Aultbea, Wester Ross, IV22 2HU
Tel: +44(0)1445 731242
www.lochewedistillery.co.uk/whisky-experience

The Whisky School at Springbank
85 Longrow, Campbeltown, Argyll, PA28 6EX
Tel: +44(0)1586 552009
whiskyschool@springbankwhisky.com

The Spirit of Speyside Whisky School takes place as a part of The Spirit of Speyside Whisky Festival. The school takes place at various distilleries over its three-day duration.
www.spiritofspeyside.com/whiskyschool

Scotch Whisky Trail Courses
Glasgow Metropolitan College, 60 North Hanover St, Glasgow, Scotland G1 2BP Tel: +44(0)1415 566222
www.glasgowmet.ac.uk/the-whisky-trail

Scotch Whisky Research Center
Branches across Japan, including Tokyo and Osaka, with 2,000 students graduating each year.
www.scotchclub.org

Societies and contacts

For more information about whiskey, and to share your appreciation with others, there are a number of international societies you can join.

Companions of the Quaich (Canada) www.thequaich.com

Bardstown Bourbon Society
www.bardstownwhiskeysociety.com

The Scotch Malt Whisky Society of America
www.smwsa.com

The Bureau of Malt Sippers (USA)
www.scotch-tasting-bums.com/welcome

The Whisky Guild (USA)
www.whiskyguild.com/whiskynetwork/home

Los Angeles Whiskey Society www.lawhiskeysociety.com

The Malt Society Boston www.maltsociety.com

For other useful sources of information, try the following list of websites, forums, and blogs:

The Scotch Whisky Association
www.scotch-whisky.org.uk

Kentucky Bourbon Trail www.kybourbontrail.com

Scotch Whisky.net www.scotchwhisky.net

Whisky Whisky Whisky
www.whiskywhiskywhisky.com

John Hansell, the editor of The Malt Advocate
www.whatdoesjohnknow.com

The Bladnoch Forum
www.bladnoch.co.uk/threads/ubbthreads

The Malt Maniacs www.maltmaniacs.org

Straight Bourbon www.straightbourbon.com

Ralf Mitchell's blog www.ralfy.com

Whiskey Professor www.whiskeyprof.com

Glossary

Angels' share As a cask of whiskey matures, it loses liquid content and alcoholic strength through evaporation. The generally accepted (by H.M. Customs & Excise) loss is 2% per annum, although a small cask in a warmer area will lose much more.

Aqua vitae The Latin words meaning "water of life."

Backset see sour mash

Beer still The first still in American whiskey production, equivalent to the wash still in Scotch or Irish production.

Broker A business that buys casks from a distiller and sells them on to a blender or independent bottler. Many brokers are now also independent bottlers themselves.

Cask strength The strength at which the whiskey comes out of the cask(s) in which it has been aging.

Chill-filtration The removal of certain fats and tartrates (and also a little flavor) from the spirit at bottling by reducing the temperature to 25°F before bottling. This ensures that the whiskey is always clear and clean.

Direct fired Most stills nowadays are heated by steam-filled coils within the still. Historically, they were direct fired, or heated by a fire lit underneath the still.

Draff The solids remaining in the mash tun after the wort has been drained off. Draff is a high-protein cattle fodder.

Finish The practice of finalizing a whiskey's maturation by filling the whisk(e)y into a different cask for the last period of its aging.

Green malt The barley grain when it has been germinated.

Grist The mixture of flour and husk ground from the dried green malt and cooked grains.

Low wines The output from the first distillation in a pot still distillation, generally around 20% a.b.v.

Lyne arm The tube, attached to the top of a pot still, that carries the evaporate into a condenser or a worm tub.

Make The general term given to the spirit produced in a distillery.

Mash The porridge-like mixture of grist and water that is heated to produce wort.

Mash bill Grain recipe used by American distillers.

Pagoda heads The distinctive feature on the roof of malt whisky distilleries. Nowadays, many are merely decorative, but their initial purpose was to draw the smoke up through the grain being dried in a kiln.

Peat Soil, containing a high level of decaying vegetable matter that, when dried, is used as a fuel. In whisky terms, it is used as a fuel, which adds the smoky flavor to the spirit.

Pot ale The liquid remaining in the wash still after the low wines have been drawn off. Also known as "burnt ale," it is dried and used as animal fodder.

Scottish Malt Distillers The malt distilling arm of The Distillers Company Limited, the forerunner to Diageo plc.

Small batch Traditional definition: a bourbon that is produced/distilled in small quantities of approximately 1,000 gallons or less (20 barrels) from a mash bill of around 200 bushels of grain.

Sour mash The habit of retaining a portion of the previous fermentation batch, together with its live yeast cells, which is added to the next run of mash, together with fresh yeast. This helps the brewer to retain a consistent character in their wash.

Spent lees Wash without alcohol, i.e. water and solids.

Staves The strips of wood that make up the sides of a barrel or cask.

Top dressing A single whiskey of high quality, the addition of which to a blend raises the flavor of that blend to a higher level.

Uisge baugh From the Scots Gaelic, meaning literally "the water of life," but the spirit drunk pre-mid-18th century and generally mixed with herbs and/or spices to make a coarse spirit more palatable.

Uisge beatha The Scots Gaelic "water of life" drunk on its own or with a little water.

Uisce beatha The Irish Gaelic equivalent.

Wash The liquid obtained by fermenting wort with yeast, basically a high alcohol, hop-less beer that is destined for distillation in the wash still.

Wort The hot, sweet liquid drawn off the draff in the mash tun, containing all the sugars from the grains.

Worm tubs A large tub outside a distillery into which a coiled copper tube of decreasing diameter attached to the lyne arm of a pot still (the worm) sits. The worm tub contains running cold water and, inside it, the evaporate from the still condenses.

Index

143